Thomas Thellusson Carter

Spiritual instructions on the Holy Eucharist

Second Edition

Thomas Thellusson Carter

Spiritual instructions on the Holy Eucharist
Second Edition

ISBN/EAN: 9783337280086

Printed in Europe, USA, Canada, Australia, Japan

Cover: Foto ©Lupo / pixelio.de

More available books at **www.hansebooks.com**

SPIRITUAL INSTRUCTIONS

ON

The Holy Eucharist.

BY THE
REV. T. T. CARTER,
RECTOR OF CLEWER.

Second Edition.

LONDON:
JOSEPH MASTERS, 78, NEW BOND STREET.
NEW YORK: POTT AND AMERY.
MDCCCLXXI.

LONDON:
PRINTED BY J. MASTERS AND SON,
ALBION BUILDINGS, BARTHOLOMEW CLOSE, E.C.

TO THE

SUPERIOR AND SISTERS

OF

The Community of S. John Baptist,

A MEMORIAL OF THANKFULNESS TO GOD FOR HAVING BEEN
PERMITTED TO MINISTER TO THEM FOR A
SPACE OF NEARLY TWENTY YEARS,

THESE INSTRUCTIONS,

ORIGINALLY PREPARED FOR THEIR USE,

ARE

VERY AFFECTIONATELY

DEDICATED.

Greatly as the Church in our land is already indebted to the venerable and beloved author of this book, we doubt whether all that he has hitherto written will exercise so powerful an influence for good, or cause the greatest verities of the faith to sink down so deep into the heart, as these "Instructions on the Holy Eucharist." When you read them they seem to breathe around them the very atmosphere of heaven. "They were not intended," Mr. Carter tell us, "to present a systematic view of the mystery of which they treat.......... The purpose contemplated was rather to cherish devotion and suggest materials for meditation."

PREFACE.

The following Addresses were not intended to present a systematic view of the Mystery of which they treat, nor were the subjects selected on any definite plan. The purpose contemplated was rather to cherish devotion and suggest materials for meditation; and the subjects were chosen as circumstances seemed to suggest. The Reader is requested to bear this explanation in mind, as some apology for any want of order in the arrangement, and for repetitions which it is feared may be found to exist.

The Addresses were given to the Sisters of the Community of S. John Baptist, in the Chapel of the House of Mercy at Clewer, for their special use. But it is hoped that they may be found useful in a wider sphere than that for which they were originally intended. At the same time their primary object needs to be borne in mind, because the sentiments and advices often have a special reference to a Sister's life, and are therefore generally applicable only with certain modifications.

The Addresses were taken down at the time of delivery, and from the notes then made have been reproduced as correctly as was possible in a permanent shape. Should the mode of treatment be found helpful, other subjects, which have formed the matter of similar instruction, may hereafter be prepared for publication.

In the Second Edition the title of the 14th Instruction, not the Instruction itself, has been changed. The only other alteration is the addition of fresh sentences in different parts, which had been found to have been omitted in the first writing of these Instructions from the notes.

T. T. C.

CONTENTS.

		PAGE
I.	THE MANIFESTATION	1
II.	THE TRANSFORMATION	11
III.	THE TRANSFORMATION (*continued*)	20
IV.	THE UNFOLDING LIFE	30
V.	THE LAW OF PROGRESS	38
VI.	THE FRUIT OF LOVE	49
VII.	SPIRITUAL AND SACRAMENTAL COMMUNION	61
VIII.	THE SINLESS LIFE	71
IX.	THE SACRIFICE	82
X.	THE SACRIFICE (*continued*)	96
XI.	THE DIVINE MISSION	107
XII.	THE RETREAT ON THE MOUNT	119
XIII.	THE REPOSE OF FAITH	130
XIV.	THE WORSHIP OF THE DIVINE PRESENCE	146
XV.	THE INCARNATION ILLUSTRATED	156
XVI.	THE MINISTRY OF THE HOLY SPIRIT	166
XVII.	THE FULNESS OF THE SACRAMENTAL LIFE	176

THE HOLY EUCHARIST.

I.

THE MANIFESTATION.

THE Commemoration of the Institution of the Holy Eucharist is unlike the great Festivals relating to our Blessed LORD in one important respect. While recalling the past, it ever renews it, causing it to be still actually present. Its commemoration is historical, because it is a true remembrance of a past event in our LORD's history. But it does far more. It brings back the event which it recalls; it has power to make it an ever living reality. The act of consecration which first took place in the Upper Chamber, is renewed again and again, as living, as life-giving, as ever in every fresh commemoration. The same supernatural Presence is before us again and again as real and true as when first vouchsafed in the "same night in which He was betrayed." The same Offering is renewed again and again with unceasing efficacy. The same Gift is bestowed. Each fresh Eucharist is not merely a commemoration; it is rather a continuation, a renewed, perpetual manifestation in the very same order of supernatural life, of the vivid truth of the same mysterious action by the same Hand of the Same LORD, Himself still actively present, still ministering, in the midst of us.

The annual Commemoration of the Institution of the Blessed Sacrament as commonly observed in the West, Corpus Christi Day, follows in natural and fit succession after the greater Festivals of the Incarnation; for it is the fulfilment of the end to which they looked in this our present life. JESUS was conceived, and born, and lived, and offered Himself up, and rose again, and ascended to take possession of His throne in glory, and sent forth His Spirit,—the object of this stupendous series of ineffable mercies being that He might be closely united with His elect, giving Himself to them to abide in them. This union, this giving of Himself, as the end of all that went before, is accomplished through this very sacramental Presence. The Holy Eucharist is thus the consummation on earth of all the mysteries of our LORD's previous life, the fulfilment of the progressive events of the whole dispensation of the Incarnation. The institution of the Blessed Sacrament was the gathering up, and closing, as to our earthly state, of all His purposes in coming; for He came to enter into our nature. His suffering in our nature, His glorification in our nature, had this for their proper end,—His own repose in actual personal Presence in His Own mystical Body of which we are members, and therefore in ourselves.

Through this Mystery our LORD accomplishes His purpose of bringing us into union with Himself, and with the FATHER in Himself. Whatever had gone before in His life or sufferings, has its accomplishment in this realisation of the desired union of the Divine and human natures, of the Creator and the creature, perpetuated and sealed in the Blessed Sacrament. The result is the perfecting of Divine Love. And Love, the perfection of all Divine manifestations, stands out as if alone in this mystical commemoration. Almighty power is withdrawn from view. The Divine Justice, to the demands of which our Lord submitted Himself in the Sacrifice of the Cross, ceases to urge its claims on Him or us. His Infiniteness has contracted Itself, and, for our sakes, subjects Itself to finite laws of space and time. His Immensity has reconciled Itself to our littleness; the light of His glory to our dimness of sight. All has given way to make room for the one yearning of Divine Love to impart Himself, at any cost of self-abnegation,—to unite Himself with the creature, to rest in this perfect union, to communicate all His purity, all His sweetness, all His Beatitude, in one act of inconceivably condescending mercy.

The Holy Eucharist is, moreover, an entirely new mode of manifestation, one peculiar to itself, different from any that had gone before. The secret longing for the revelation of God which had prevailed among the Faithful for ages before the Incarnation, here finds at last its true response. Such words as these,—"Thou that sittest between the Cherubim, show Thyself;" "Show the light of Thy Countenance and we shall be whole;"—were the ceaseless expressions of desire felt by the faithful of earlier days, for what might at once enkindle light in the soul, and satisfy its cravings and its needs with the healing power and grace of a supernatural sanctity. The most saintly living during that long period, knew only the forecasting of a blessedness that has now at length found a home on earth. Theirs was a time of prophetic breathings, a prolonged period of desires. This is ended, for the realisation of these desires is now the daily Food of the Faithful.

When at last God took our nature, His Godhead was still shrouded in completest secrecy, His Humanity alone being palpable to outward sight and outward touch. After a while even that Manifestation passed away; even His Human Form was withdrawn. There was then a real absence, a real void; but during this brief interval there was kindled in the hearts of His disciples a more intense expectation, alive with a more entire assurance; for the Lord Himself had been seen, and had promised to return quickly. During the interval of the great forty days there was no Communion. During the ten days that followed His Ascension there was still no Communion. Nor could there be, for there was no Real Presence. Our Lord's Humanity was assuming, during that period, a new and more glorious state, in which He was becoming capable of a new form of Manifestation. His Human Nature was being more perfectly spiritualized, exalted into the highest glory in union with Infinite Godhead, invested with new attributes, that in the descending of the Holy Ghost He might be able to give Himself forth in an infinite self-communication, to be indeed hidden still, but present as He had never been before, and received as He could not have been before,— His Body and His Blood capable of being present on every altar of the Catholic Church before the longing eyes of His faithful ones; His Humanity hidden equally as His Deity, His entire Person wholly secret, though assuredly there present, and yet mystically revealed to a new consciousness, which was to become the property of His own elect, the new sense of faith made capable of communicating with His new mode of Presence.

Hence there flow out all the consequences which we now perceive in ourselves, in our innermost being, after the reception of the Blessed Sacrament. There is then a fulness, a satisfying rapt joy, a pervading sweetness, a springing of a new life, taking us out of ourselves, transforming us in a mode peculiar to that hour. This exulting consciousness is caused by the fact, that there has passed into us our LORD's secret Presence in His very Flesh, in a nature kindred with our own, heavenly and joyous as the Spirit's Presence, yet unlike it—more sensibly felt, more penetrating, more absorbing, melting, as it were, into Himself our whole susceptible being, in a way in which our LORD alone can effect us, because He alone is of the same nature with us, and thus can alone perfectly unite Himself with us, so to possess us that we may be wholly one with Him.

O Mystery! beyond reach even of the spiritual understanding, however illuminated, which the ceaseless operations of Divine power and love through such long ages conspired to accomplish—a real Communion with the Living GOD, the assimilating of the Heavenly Substance with our own in a oneness of eternal life, the Infinite, the Ancient of Days, coalescing in loving harmony with the finite, the creature of an hour! What a view does it exhibit of the spirituality of the life into which we pass! All we are,—spirit and body, flesh and blood, every thought, every feeling, every organ, every faculty in us, becomes the seat of GOD's mysterious Presence. He, indwelling wholly within us, comes, as we receive Him, to spiritualize every thought, feeling, faculty in us like unto Himself. All that is of nature in us through this union with Him, is gifted with grace to become heavenly; all of self to pass into GOD; all the human to be identified with the Divine, the life of the creature assimilated to the Life of the Eternal Godhead. It is thus He comes transformed that He may transform us. Our LORD's own life in the flesh marks assuredly the tone, the character of the life which thenceforward must be ours. We must after His example discipline our life by secret mortification, by overcoming self, by doing away all impurity, by subduing all that is of nature, all that is of the world, all that is of self. Our spirits must be sublimed, our thoughts, feelings, desires, imaginations, words, looks, movements, more and more must assume the character of that heavenly state in which alone our LORD can abide, and rest, and be satisfied.

As in our LORD so in us there must be a real hiddenness. His Presence in the Blessed Sacrament is wholly withdrawn from all outward sense, to be perceived only by the higher consciousness of pure faith, the highest spiritual perception. There is, as already observed, no sensible or material manifestation, nothing outward. All that was once visible is withdrawn, inscrutably hidden, even as His Deity was hidden during His earthly sojourn,—withdrawn in union with the FATHER; and this hidden Presence should mark the manner of our life, as we seek to imitate Him, as we become one with Him. Our inner life must grow into this His present life in us, losing more and more all consciousness of self, all desire of being observed, noticed, spoken of, thought about, cared for, considered—that we may be withdrawn, even as He is; lost in GOD; self not stirring, because absorbed in the higher sense of being only in Him, under His care, gathered up in His love, dying with Him, rising again with Him, more and more associated, united with Him: He All in us, we all in Him.

Again, His Presence in this Divine Manifestation is most wonderfully marked by repose and silence. The Blessed Sacrament is the very centre of rest, the very secret shrine of quietness. All around the altar is suffused, filled, saturated with the same wondrous unearthly stillness. Nowhere on earth, as in this charmed circle, do we feel so still a calm. It is because our LORD is there perceived secretly abiding, and felt to be diffusing around Him His own ineffable peace, the calmness of His wondrous Presence. This, too, should mark our life, for as we receive our LORD, we receive Him in this same calmness. We are conformed to Him in proportion as our own lives grow in quietness, His peace spreading within our own souls. Even amid all that outwardly disturbs us, we have, if we have Him, the same peace, because He is Peace, sustained and sustaining our whole being.

But how greatly, how continually do we fail to carry out what it is manifestly intended we should become, through participation of CHRIST, in this Blessed Communion! How often do we resolve, pledge ourselves, as we receive Him, to take Him to be our Master; tell Him that He shall rule us, that we will have no other LORD, that His Law shall be our life, if He will but give Himself to reign over us; that His rule in us shall be supreme, that He shall be Lord, King, in the very fulness of power! He comes, He seats Himself on the throne of our hearts. He accepts our promise, He owns our desire, He takes us at our word. But how continually do we, and this too, alas! so quickly, forget our pledges, withdraw this homage, and let ourselves be sold at will to be under another's dominion, losing all the consciousness of the gentle sweetness, the loving sway which pervaded our hearts, when we made the covenant with Him; thus failing Him when He most needs us, deaf to His voice, when He speaks the first word of command, if it be against our own will, or the prevailing desire of our souls, and readily sinking under some miserable temptation, which has quickly overmastered what seemed His perfect reign within us.

How often, as we approached the altar, have we resolved, that if He came to us we would take Him as our model and our example, that we would keep His Life before us, and copy It, and transcribe It upon our souls! He comes, He reveals to us His perfect Law, His beauty of saintliness. He is before us, within us, we are rejoiced, we go forth enraptured. Suddenly an unexpected trial comes, it may be but a slight disturbance troubles us, and His example is instantly forgotten. We have given way; we have gone against His clearest teaching; we have turned from the very thought of copying His glorious Life, though it may have been but in the early morning that we pledged ourselves to keep it before us as our constant aim, and the morning has not yet deepened into day when we failed Him.

How often, e.g., when we received Him, have we resolved to live a mortified and restrained life in the fresh delighted power with which He had strengthened us! But quickly have we fallen back into the very same habits of self-indulgence which before had saddened us, and led us in sorrow to confess our shame.

Even when the effort has been urged upon us, the possible mortification pointed out, we have shrunk back from it, and yielded ourselves to the softer way of some self-pleasing course; all our promises broken, the old subtle habits of our natural life again overruling us.

How often have we resolved that, if our LORD would thus come and be with us, and abide in us, we would keep up the same recollection; preserve it as our blessedness, our joy, our security, aiming always at the standard we felt, we saw before us as we knelt at the altar. But the impulses of self have been quickly stirred again. Distractions have unsteadied us. Our activities have carried us away. How rapidly, how entirely sometimes the consciousness of union has passed, become wholly lost to us, as though it had never been!

How, then, must He be grieved! How sorely disappointed! How ashamed of His faithful one's unworthiness! How does He record against us, that the early morning promise was but like the morning dew! How often has this been so! How wonderful that our LORD continues still to be ours, to give Himself to us as at the beginning; to bear with us through all our changes, all our fitful fluctuations, all our falseness! For He abides with us ever the Same, He changes not. How graciously, how mysteriously merciful! He still holds to us, clings to us, through all disappointments, keeps us for Himself, and Himself for us, ever patient, ever waiting the convenient season, waiting for our, not His, willingness. He is ever drawing us, inclining us, turning us to be more and more faithful, that at last commemorating the mystery of His glory, with exceeding joy and thankfulness we may truly, unreservedly yield ourselves up to do His will, that the perfect blessedness of this Divine Sacrament may be ours, by securing its fulness of bliss, even after so long a period of faithlessness, and coldness and untruth.

Help us, O most Merciful! Add to all Thy other gifts this further grace, without which all would be as nothing, that we may have increasing capacity to receive Thee, steadfastness to follow Thee, feeding on the opening Vision, till at last we shall see Thee unveiled face to face; still for a little while hidden, but at length seen in Thy fulness of glory, and ourselves made for ever one with Thee, as Thou art One with the FATHER, in the light that can never fade, never fail us. Amen.

II.

THE TRANSFORMATION.

It has pleased God to impart His perfect Life, His own Divine Nature to His Elect, but not directly from His pure Godhead. He has made the Humanity of our Lord the medium of this perfect life. His Flesh is become the shrine in which the fulness of the Godhead dwells bodily, and out of which, and through which, the inner life of Deity, the glory of His otherwise unapproachable Nature passes, and is communicated, so accommodated to our frailty, that we may partake in our measure of the Divine perfections. The Holy Eucharist is the actual present centre on earth of this life, the abode of this Life-giving power of God; the well-spring whence flow the streams of all healing virtue and grace.

We adore our Lord mystically present, as on His Throne, upon the Altar in the Majesty of His Sanctity, as the Lord and Giver of this new and supernatural Life, glorified, and glorifying His Elect in His amazing purpose of thus becoming one with them. We adore Him in this Mystery as the author of our Perfection, the All-Holy Fount of our complete sanctification. He is there divested of all that marred His appearance in the Flesh during His earthly humiliation. There is nothing in Him there of toil or suffering, no outward expression of anguish, nothing of the agony, of the pain of the sacrifice; no marks of the scorn, the shame He bore in the days of His ministry, nothing of sorrow, no cry of human bitterness, such as was heard on the Cross when He won for the world that redemption so dearly purchased. But here before us in the Blessed Sacrament we have the results of all that awful distress, all the consequences emanating from that life of unutterable Sorrow. He is now beyond the possible reach of pain or insult, because sin has done its worst; because, as a true scapegoat, He bore it far away, and, unlike the symbolic victim, to return freed from its power for ever, having cast it off as He triumphed over it in Death; and now He is passed beyond its reach into heaven unto GOD. "In that He died, He died unto sin once, but in that He liveth, He liveth unto GOD."

The adoration we pay Him now in His Presence on the Altar, is a reparation for all the insults, and the marring, and the shame, which He was contented once all silently to bear. It is the offering which the grateful Church perpetually offers to Him, where around Him all is pure love, all peace, all undimmed beauty, all saving virtue. We adore Him there revealed to faith with a calm and restful gratitude, remembering His past sorrows, and rejoicing in His present ineffable, inconceivable joy. Our Adoration is to Him the satisfaction of His soul, the offering up of a sweet savour well pleasing in His sight, as the best recompense of contrite Humanity sorrowing over the storm of rage and malignity, which once rose and beat upon Him on earth, now changed into the calm light of the splendour of His Holiness in which He reigns for ever. We recognize Him here only under this aspect of miraculous power to heal, of ceaseless outpourings of Divine grace, of the blessedness of the Divine perfections manifested in the Flesh.

Most marvellous, how in such a Presence of Power and Holiness our LORD can adapt Himself to what He finds in us! We could not dare to draw near as often as we do to worship Him, to receive Him into us, were it not for this mysterious adaptation and condescension which tempers the full radiance of His Glory in His veiled Presence. He is present in His whole Person, undivided, indivisible, His Divinity, His Humanity, with all the treasures of His grace, all the virtues of His Sacred Passion, all the might of His infinite Godhead,—all are before us. Where the one portion of His Being and His Attributes is, there the others must needs be; for He cannot be divided. He Himself is One, and He, in the entirety of His Glory and Power, is there hidden, yet most truly *there*. The Mystery which we believe is this,—that without losing aught of His own separate Glory, He adapts that which is boundless to that which He finds within us, however contracted, that which is perfect to that which is miserable and feeble, accommodates Himself to whatever He finds within us. We could not receive Him and live, if it were not so. We could not bear the burden of His greatness, unless He so condescended to our incapacity and weakness. So secret is His Presence, that He withdraws from our consciousness all that He really is, even while we receive Him in His fulness, lest we should be overwhelmed. It is a great and signal part of His mercy to hide His Majesty, in which He passes into us. So wonderful is His tenderness and condescension, even to the least and unworthiest, that He can wait till we are prepared, and has so ordered His gift of Himself that, in proportion to what we are, He gives out from Himself what He enables us to receive, and no more. Whatever, according to our measure, of spirituality we can digest and assimilate—what will turn to our health, and not to our hurt, He imparts. He restrains Himself, till there is a capacity to receive Him; and then gives in proportion to our capacity. He holds back from our view what we are incapable of apprehending; and as we come again and again with enlarged desires for His grace, He also enlarges the outpouring of His gift to transform and sanctify us. Again and again there flashes across the soul some fresh sight leading us on, and as we attain the object of our increased longing, He shows us still height beyond height, that ever being drawn upward we may be filled with an ever-growing measure of His Fulness. Thus gradually we advance, because He gradually unfolds the secrets of His treasures. Thus He inspires the longings which He purposes to satisfy; and as He satisfies, He ever more and more developes new capacities to correspond with new manifestations of the opening visions of His perfections.

And yet we do indeed always actually receive our LORD and our GOD, as He alone can be received, in His Fulness; and we take Him, and He enters into us, in His whole Presence, entire, undivided. If we could but once apprehend Him as He apprehends us, the fulfilment of His most gracious purpose in coming to us would be at once accomplished. Couldest thou wholly die, He Himself would wholly live in thee, and thou couldest say in very truth, as S. Paul, after his long and patient life of grace, was enabled to say: " It is no longer I that live, but CHRIST liveth in me; and the life I now live in the flesh, I live by faith in the SON of GOD, who loved me, and gave Himself for me."[1] Could there be within thee the death of every movement that is merely thy own, every strong impulse of the fulness of All that is His would take its place, thou wouldest be transubstantiated in thyself—thy own substance no more, His Substance become wholly thine; or rather thy substance, still existing though changed, would be transformed into His Substance, and Himself become the only Ruler and LORD of thy life. We receive Him in power to effect this. We receive Him in all His attributes. His Being in His eternal Deity before time was, so far as is possible, is communicated to the creature; what has passed upon Him in His Incarnation, His Conception, His life in the flesh, His ministry, His long endurance, His labours and miracles of healing, His transfiguration, His Passion, His Death, His Resurrection, His Ascension, His Session at the Right hand of the FATHER, His giving forth of the HOLY SPIRIT, His whole collected, combined virtues and graces,—all that the FATHER has shed upon Him as the consequence of His accepted sacrifice, every gift, every energy and breathing of the perfect Life in Humanity which He took, not for Himself, but for us;— all are in us in that hour, because He is in us, and because we dwell in Him, and He dwells in us.

Consider, then, how much depends on the state in which we approach. Practically our LORD is within us only in proportion as we are prepared to co-operate. The measure of His Fulness is adapted to the measure of our capacity. He co-operates with us as we co-operate with Him; He yields Himself, and gives out of

[1] Gal. ii. 10.

Himself, in correspondence with our will and desires. His Life is whole and perfect in us, so far as He Himself and His purpose for us are concerned. But It can only slowly advance, because we only slowly correspond with It. We only yield ourselves by degrees, and so He can only communicate by degrees all that is already ours in the possibilities of the unrestrained Fulness of His Indwelling.

Most marvellous mystery of Love! Beyond the Gift Itself is this condescension, this patient waiting, this longsuffering, this accommodation, this tempering of His Glory. He is the Same LORD yesterday, to-day, and for ever, wherever He is, only His transformation of us in Himself differs,—the Same on His Throne in Heaven, the Same in His Blessed Sacrament, the Same when enshrined in our hearts, only different in His manifestation; and the mystery of His Fulness varies in His Presence in us only because we vary in our power of partaking of Him.

Consider what our lives would be if, through an active co-operation with our LORD, we were faithful to our mysterious possession of Him. What an unfolding of wondrous light, in thought, in word, in deed, in aspiration, in design, would characterize our inward nature! What a consciousness would pervade us! What an upholding strength sustain us! What a companionship be felt within, what communing with our unseen Guest, if only we could always bear in mind what it is to receive GOD; could think and feel and act in conformity with the conviction of His indwelling Presence, possessing and possessed, though hidden under an inscrutable veil, screened from all mortal sense!

It is not that we lose anything of our own true nature through this mysterious transformation, we are still our own true selves. Our individuality and special characteristics of being remain. All that is truly ours only becomes more intensely ours, for our true nature becomes more real. The only change is that our nature is pervaded by a life and love beyond it, transforming it into a diviner order ever more and more perfectly. And as our efforts prevail to preserve a life of stillness and repose, of faith and love, of prayer and watchfulness, and a pure intention, this diviner life in us is increasingly strengthened and enlarged. All is transformed and raised, as more and more we unite ourselves with the amazing Mystery of the Presence Which is inhabiting our being, working out its purposes in us, and which is already ours in Its immeasurable inexhaustible depth of love.

Again, consider what our life ought to become in its intercourse with others. Should not we be to others what our LORD is to us? He is, as He possesses us, the centre of healing virtue and power, diffusing Himself in a pure spirituality throughout the nature which He has for this end rescued from death, and associated with Himself. If this be His purpose in His Sacramental Presence, should not we in this world be in our converse with others a like source of healing and of love? If the intended results of His communications were carried out, should we not speak, and act, and think, towards the outward world, as CHRIST speaks to us in our own hearts? Nature would cease to influence us; natural actings would die down in us. All our thoughts and plans, our words and efforts, would be constrained to move after that higher law, which is one with the law of His own perfected life. Our conversation would be

Christ working in us, even as our inward life would be Christ living in us. Our law of dealing in our mutual intercourse with others would be in the same love and beneficence in which He gives Himself to us, in which He diffuses Himself within our hearts. The Life that is in us would radiate from us; we should become, by grace, centres of a Divine activity, peculiar manifestations of saving influence, channels through which the life of God would spread. We should win the blessing of being co-operators with Him in the shining forth of the Light of His love towards men, that the Father through Him, and in Him through us, might be the more glorified.

And yet, while thus possessing and possessed of God, how continually do we speak and act through some mere carnal impulse, some passing disturbance or irregularity, speaking, acting, merely as of ourselves, of our own mere natural spirit! And this notwithstanding our own experience has taught us, that such efforts can never touch souls, can never influence, can never win sympathy; for nature resists nature, the natural powers of life on which we seek to act by a kindred power instinctively rise in self-defence, refusing to yield to what is no greater or better than themselves. Hearts will only yield to God. They can only be touched by His Love, they will be moved only by the saving virtues of His Passion. So that words and actions are spent in vain unless instinct with the grace that flows from Christ, unless we bring to bear the powers derived from His Presence, to be transmitted, through our agency, to those to whom He intended it to pass, if we are willing to be the honoured instruments of His gracious operations.

Only when we thus speak and act in the consciousness of His Power, of His indwelling Life, as He lives and moves and breathes in us, can we hope for success in winning and swaying other souls. Nature yields to Him, to the manifestation of His sacred Presence, acknowledging its LORD. In the sensible going forth of His power there is a subduing, softening influence, a felt power of GOD, even through weakest instruments.

O wonderful grace and love of the Life-giving GOD! May we know the glory which Thou willest us to share with Thee, that we may be able to kindle the fire of love in the breasts of others through the manifestation of Thyself, saving others even as we ourselves are saved!

We need to seek earnestly, that we fail not to attain all that may thus become ours, passing into us out of His fulness; that we may rise even to the measure of the stature of CHRIST. He will surely meet us with His response of love, if we thus ask and seek. He will not restrain Himself, if we are not restrained. It is His gift, though we must seek it. His Hand is not shortened, He can save to the uttermost all that come unto the FATHER by Him, and the FATHER is ever drawing us to Him, that we may be His crown of rejoicing in His day. Then, when He is no longer unseen, seated on the Throne of His glory with all His Saints gathered around Him as monuments of His grace, manifestations of His power, we shall find our place predestined for us in His love, to be for ever at rest in Him, our work accomplished, all its weariness and toil past, and, instinct with the fulness of preternatural energy, bearing our part in the adoration which arises around Him from the heavenly Host for ever and ever.

III.

THE TRANSFORMATION (*continued.*)

From our Lord's Presence in the Blessed Sacrament of the Altar, we derive special indications of the true character of our transformation in God. For the mystery is full of practical applications as to the qualities of grace in which we are to resemble God, and hold intimate living communion with Him, because He therein exhibits Himself as the Teacher and Model, as well as the Feeder of His Faithful ones. Not only do we there receive the increase of spiritual life: we also learn the characteristics of the life which He wills us to acquire, the direction which it should take, the laws by which it grows.

There are three different aspects under which our Blessed Lord's Life in His Sacramental Presence is to be viewed, or three modes in which more especially He therein manifests Himself.

There is, (1,) His Life towards the Father; (2,) His Life within itself; and (3,) His Life towards us. Under each of these aspects of our Lord's Sacramental life, practical lessons may be drawn as to our own.

(1.) There is the perpetual intercession before the Father for His own elect, in ceaseless love pleading for us; the constant presentation of Himself as a victim, by Himself as a Priest, offering for sin, pleading His sacrifice, as He bears His people in His heart, seeking for them forgiveness and the outpourings of all His powers to save. There too in His Humanity He adores the FATHER, on Whom He ever gazes, still absorbed in the longing, which on earth as a fire consumed Him, of increasing the glory of His FATHER, by winning and perfecting the souls whom the FATHER's love draws to Him. This intent direction of His thought to the FATHER, as the object of adoration, of atoning love, of ceaseless prayer, is as prominent a feature of our LORD's Sacramental Presence, as it was of His ministry in the days of His Flesh.

(2.) His own Life, in itself, is on the other hand completely changed. There was from His infancy a constant onward progress, a continual increase, a growing, a perfecting of the Manhood in GOD through appointed transitions, according to laws pre-ordained for the full completeness of His Incarnation, that He might be made in all things like unto us, sin only except. This onward change was wrought through trial, suffering and effort; through outward affliction, and inward pain; through an awful death; through the grave; through the transfiguration wrought in His Resurrection into the glory which He willed at last to assume, and even then still by degrees, as He ascended upwards into the innermost Heavens, to take His place upon His Throne on the Right Hand of His FATHER. All these transitions have been passed through, and in the fulness of His perfected Humanity, all now is repose. Enshrined in the glory of its own true home, Humanity abides in perfect peace, One with the Everlasting, Infinite Godhead, in unutterable, ineffable bliss, as the rest which followed the weary toil of His accomplished

Passion. His life in His Sacrament is One with His life at the Right Hand of His FATHER, beyond the reach of change, or the fluctuations of time, or outward disturbance, in stillness and profound peace, not as in the earlier stages of the Incarnation.

(3.) Again, towards ourselves, now, as ever before, His life is one prolonged act of self-sacrifice. He comes to us to communicate Himself, to give out of Himself the life which He has won for us, and which He has made through His Spirit capable of being imparted beyond Himself to whomsoever He will. The desire of thus imparting, thus giving Himself, makes Him assume this mysterious secrecy, this silent hidden Presence in these lowly forms of the earthly creatures, utterly unworthy of His true dignity, but suitable to us as true symbols of His marvellous gifts of life and refreshment, capable of most wonderful assimilation with us as our food, because He would interpenetrate us, spirit, soul, and body, in one abounding flood of life, one gush of eternal spirituality to thrill through all the being of His Beloved, His own Elect.

Under these aspects of our Blessed LORD's life in His Eucharistic Presence, we see laws binding upon ourselves, as we grow into a Sacramental Life, and It becomes more and more the copy of His own. The resemblance is perfected, as we are transformed according to these same laws of life.

(1.) Thus one aspect of our life should ever turn towards the FATHER. What is recorded of the Holy Angels who minister around the children of GOD on earth, that they always "behold the Face of their FATHER Which is in Heaven," is pre-eminently the characteristic of those who live a sacramental life in union with JESUS, both for their own sake, and for the sake of others. For their own sake, because they are ever adoring Him, ever pleading with Him, laying before Him their cares, their anxieties, their needs, their temptations, their weaknesses, their secret conflicts, their sins, their aspirations,—all that forms the distress and conflict of their life, while they seek cleansing, power, deliverance, consolation, light, rest. For the sake of others, the same ceaseless pleading must arise, specially from those who bear the burden of others' lives as well as their own,—the bringing before GOD their necessities, their cares, their trials, endeavouring to win grace and power and peace for all, according to their need.

(2.) Again, the repose, the quiet balanced rest which marks our LORD's perfected life, is intended to grow more and more steadfast in those who are truly His, not the repose of indolence, not the calm arising from absence of trial or the lack of temptation, a mere accidental freedom from inward struggle or difficulty, but the repose which lives in the mortification of desire, in the conquest of passion, in the crucifixion of self, in a subdued will, in the reconciliation of every thought with a perfected obedience, as the whole inner being, entranced in GOD, yields itself in delighted harmony with His perfect Mind. Such repose is attained through the continual progress of a life of grace, as it gradually overcomes the restlessness of nature, the excitements of self, the disturbance of temper or passion, the fruitless impatience of the will.

And again, (3,) as our LORD is a centre, diffusing life around, as He comes for the one purpose of communicating Himself to others, so there is to be also in us a resemblance to this characteristic. For that mysterious

Life, which so wonderfully enters into us to dwell in us, is given to us in order that it may become diffusive, not only passing into all the faculties and organs of our own life, but intended to make itself felt everywhere, to spread out beyond, around us, communicating itself through us to others by a sweet force manifesting itself in the outer circle of our daily life, in love and healing and manifold forms of blessing, causing others to feel that God is in us of a truth, by the effects of the higher Presence radiating from us, unknown, it may be, to ourselves, as it passes from us in tone and accent, in look or word, but yet felt by others, and testifying that we have been with Jesus, and are as Jesus in the world.

In these characteristics of life, then, like His own, our life is to grow, and in proportion as He is in us, and prevails in us, so we are transformed. We thus grow to be one with Him in the threefold aspect of His sacramental Presence. Let us consider some of the conditions on which it depends whether we may hope thus to profit by this reception of our Lord.

(1.) There is needed an elevation of soul, able to rise into communion with objects which the spirit of contemplation only can embrace, objects supernatural, beyond time and space and change, kindled with the light of another world; able also to retain the consciousness of their reality. We need to be on the mountain-top as one catching the sun's last rays, though hidden from the world below, that the light may stream into our souls, filling them, suffusing them, pervading them with its preternatural glory, an elevation of view to be sustained only by living faith embracing the vision as a substantial Presence.

(2.) With this elevation of view, this high sustained idea of possible perfection, there needs also faith in the capacity which GOD has given us to receive it. We must never allow the despairing thought, the darkness of doubt to intervene, so as to question His fulness of grace. GOD may work in whom He wills, and what He wills, and we may surely believe He will work His perfect work where He comes to dwell, not as a passing tenant, but as an abiding possessor. He will make that heart, which is to be His Home, in all things pleasing to Himself. All is possible where He wills to be in order to give life. We must needs become what He wills, in His time, however faulty and imperfect we may be in ourselves. Yea, though we may have failed a thousand times, even sinned the "seventy times seven," failed in all our resolutions and promises, He can renew our strength, rekindle our fervours, cause our death-like torpor to become the glory of His own Resurrection. His gift is Himself, given that He may enter in all His Fulness, that the soul may become the shrine of His Presence, unite with It, co-operate with It.

(3.) Again, with this elevation of mental sight, and this faith, there must be a yielded soul giving itself up to GOD, as its truer, better self; a surrender of the inmost will to be only what GOD wills, to have only what GOD gives. The reason why self has such a hold upon us is, that we have not ceased to love it. We are, therefore, still so tender over it. We cannot surrender it, because we will not. Therefore self occupies so large a part of our daily thoughts. Therefore it arises on all occasions, with every temptation. And yet to sacrifice self at any cost, any pain, is the very condition for receiving that higher, better life. How without a yielding, a giving up of our nature to be transformed, can we become the subjects of the true Lord of our hearts, when He comes to possess us? For to make us His own is to separate us from the self which cost Him His Death, which is still the continued hindrance to His perfect work.

(4.) Again, that there may be this yielding of soul in the spirit of faith, there needs yet besides a clinging recollection of that Blessed Presence which has entered in to possess us. One great cause of failure is, that we so soon forget it. Often even as we leave the altar, as our step passes beyond the sanctuary, the consciousness is gone. So changeable and fickle are our hearts, we forget Him on Whom our souls had just been feeding as our very life. One brief moment, and all has passed from us. So variable is our nature. One thought succeeds another rapidly. A passing impulse is stirred, and the whole soul is changed, and that Communion in which we had been so wrapped, so absorbed, is now afar off, is as though it had never been. Something has intervened between Him and our consciousness of His Presence. There has come a cloud, though it be of the thinnest film, but it has extinguished the sacred light, and robbed the soul of the unearthly vision. There is, then, the utmost need to endeavour to preserve a recollection of the heavenly Life we have received, to retain our hold upon It, to embrace it firmly, rejoicingly, that It may continue in our consciousness as well as in our being as the exulting choice, the Love, the Joy of our renewed life. Our prayer, as we leave the sanctuary, should be, that thus filled throughout the day with the consciousness of His abiding Presence within us, we may go forth to live in the power which now claims us as His own for ever.

(5.) It has been shown that our LORD being present to diffuse His life to all around, is the type to be fulfilled in us of a diffusiveness of love towards others. His Life only exists to diffuse Itself in Its perfect Fulness to all around. If we separate ourselves from others we mar the perfecting of the Divine Life, and check its perfect outflowing. It is the very instinct, the very purpose of the life of GOD in us to diffuse Itself, by means of ten thousand times ten thousand channels, throughout the world, throughout the whole creation. He wills to use each one who is endued with its power, as an instrument of His renewing, healing love. Therefore, if we would co-operate with this Blessed Presence, there must be with all our care, all our joy in ourselves, a generous thoughtful kindness, a real beneficent love; and this generosity of kindness, as it is the blessing of others, so it is a very special means of sustaining and enlarging the life of CHRIST within ourselves. It acts and reacts; it is its own reward. To give forth is to increase. To spend and be spent for others, is the surest increase of our own treasure. This longing, this all-pervading love, this resolved purpose that the life within may have its full, free course, must, therefore, take possession of the soul. All defects of charity must be healed. Even the smallest thought of unkindness, the least disregard for the feelings of others, is at variance with the spirit which has now passed into us. Our LORD's Presence may instantly retire back into Itself, to escape the rude touch, the jarring of any feeling alien to His nature. He must depart, if the spirit of uncharitableness prevail. Alas!

the heinousness of the sin, when that very Presence which waited for us graciously, because He was patient with us, and bore with all our sins and all our wilfulness, should find us, when He has possessed us, unwilling to bear with others' faults, full of dislikes and resentments, of envies and suspicions, of petty moroseness and distrust.

But if our course be true, our life, ever fed by our LORD within us, will be lost in GOD. Our whole nature forced from its old instincts, its active zeal raised to a higher level, will reach to a diviner thought, a holier charity, a bearing and forbearing, a perfectness of patience, in which converse with the outer world becomes already an anticipation of the communion of the saints above. Even as when the sunshine comes down in full power upon the sea, the line which marks the horizon melts into a yet brighter ray, and heaven and earth as they meet kiss each other, blending undistinguishably in perfect harmony—so our lives, in which the eternal light is shining, will be suffused with a supernatural glory, and, as we keep our destined course, our earthly state will assume the semblance of the heavenly, CHRIST transformed in us, and we all but deified in Him; our lives will be midway between heaven and earth, touching earth with our feet, while our spirits are in Heaven.

O blessed LORD! O JESU! SON of the Most High GOD! would that this infusion of heaven might be wrought in us! For this Thou didst suffer; for this Thou dost live; for this Thou dost communicate Thyself. Shall all Thy sufferings produce no result? Thy continued manifestations of Thyself, shall they be all in vain? Thy love, Thy self-sacrifice, shall it win no response? Must Thou return to Heaven after a fruitless mission? By all that Thou hast been, and art to us, dearest LORD, still give Thyself, still work mightily in us, though unworthy; make us willing in the day of Thy power. Let not Thy love be restrained, Thy power stinted. Give us of Thy healing virtue, that we may correspond with all the purposes of Thy blissful Communion; that Thou, reigning in Heaven, mayest speak of us to the FATHER, as already become one with Him through Thee, even as Thou art One with us. For this we were born again! for this we continually feed on Thee. This now we ask: that, being accepted before we go hence, Thou mayest present us to the FATHER, to be the eternal witnesses of Thy triumph, the manifestations of Thy abounding Gift; the instruments of Thy glorious work in the salvation of others, for whom, as for us, Thou, O LORD, wast content to die; that we may be found in our measure, and in our lot, links in the boundless chain of living glory, the track along which Thou hast gone before, passing into the unfathomed depth of the abyss of love in the Heart of GOD, and thus made one with Thee for ever.

IV.

THE UNFOLDING LIFE.

WE have been dwelling on the exalted character and powerful development of the Sacramental Life, intended to be infused into the soul, through participation in the Holy Eucharist. Our joy and our glory now is, that this Life in its powers and possible fulness of expansion is truly enshrined within us; that GOD, of His own Almighty, life-giving, creative energy, is increasing its actual results more and more, as the carrying out of His sure Promise; that the good work which He hath begun, He will complete in His own day, even to the full measure of the stature of CHRIST.

It is most important, lest we fall short of this promise, that each time we receive we should endeavour to keep at heart the greatness of what then passes into us, the profound mystery of which every time we are the subjects. What practically may be the result of the ever-renewed reception, we cannot measure by any present apprehension. But the mystery in which we participate on every occasion, is surely nothing less than a very death and a very resurrection. Every time we offer the Blessed Sacrifice, " we show forth the LORD's Death till He come." We commemorate, and really represent before the FATHER and before the world, the great truth of His having passed through death into

His fulness of living glory, in putting off the bonds and trammels of His earthly state, and assuming one purely spiritual and heavenly. His sufferings ceased, His last pang over, the triumph of His self-devotion attained, the completion of His Sacrifice is manifested on the Altar of Love, in the power of an endless life, as the long-desired recompense of His Passion.

If we become one with our LORD in this mystery, we too in very real though mysterious fellowship share with Him this His death and His resurrection. Every time we communicate we pass in Him through the same transformation, in which the old forms of the mere creature-life cease, and the renewed forms of the higher nature of man, one with GOD, take their place. By virtue of such communion we pass out of our earthly state into a heavenly, although the effects of the marvellous change are accomplished practically only through a long interval. Whatsoever is our own, according to the laws of nature and time and space, dies more and more; whatever is His, lives in us in ever increasing efficacy in its stead. For the moment of reception, at least, we are translated into Paradise, we are filled with Heaven, with GOD. At that great crisis, He, Whom we have received, entrances us, pervades our entire being, we are wholly His, He is wholly ours,— whether more ourselves, or more our LORD in us, we cannot tell.

It is our profoundest joy to believe, that in each reception our LORD, in His whole Life, becomes ours, in a supernatural mystery. His Sacred Heart with all its powers, whether of action or of endurance, of energy or of contemplation, of love or of peace, all enters within us, because He Himself enters within us. He has passed within us, and He is there as the LORD of our life. The fulness of all that lies hidden within that Sacred Heart, and within that Sacred Body, ever indissolubly in union with His Godhead, is in some amazing mystery within us, becomes the inner germ of our own life. He is in us. His whole Personality, as the GOD-Man, comes to abide, according to the laws of the Spirit of Holiness, in our souls and bodies.

In that Sacred Heart of JESUS are beating the perpetual pulsations of all His Love, all His thoughts of the glory of the FATHER, all His desires to save the world, all His plans for the fulfilment of the Redemption of the creature, all His inward visions, all that lives within Him,—and all this is within us, because He is within us, the Centre, the inner Life of our life. His life of peace, His boundless desires and impulses of love, of will, one with the Will of the FATHER, His ineffable Holiness, His continued unceasing actings of devotion towards His FATHER, towards each one of us, towards His whole Body, His life of intercession, His heavenly joy, are in the throbbings of His Sacred Heart, and all is in us, because He is in us.

He is acting, moving, breathing in us, for He has taken up His abode in us, and worketh in us. He gives forth His life within us as we are capable of receiving. He enlarges His gifts according to His will.

This hidden Presence, therefore, must surely characterise our lives; we must bear about us signs of this indwelling of GOD. It cannot fail to influence us, if we are recollected, if we go about in the conscious possession of this supernaturalised state. There will be proofs to show that we are believing in It, living in It, growing more and more in oneness with It. There will be such proofs as these,—

(1.) There will be a spirit of gladness, of secret, sacred joy; not that fulness of joy which will be ours hereafter, not that unintermitted unchanging beatitude which the Blessed who have attained their heavenly inheritance know, not necessarily the ecstatic state to which at times the seemingly conscious inward breathings of the HOLY GHOST impel us, lifting us up above our ordinary condition to something strange and unwonted, as though the very flood-gates of the Spirit were opened, the ocean-tide of Divine love rising within us to its higher levels—not thus necessarily, if ever; but a joy beyond this life's power either to give or take away, a life of heavenly rest which tends to become the steadfast habit of the soul, the blessed foretaste of that deep peace which passes all understanding, the fruit, O Thou Holy One of GOD, of Thy full possession of us. Surely, if we believe, if we in any manner realize the truth that GOD in a marvellous inhabitation tabernacles, as in His chosen shrine, within our being; if this truth is clear and unwavering, and has become an habitual consciousness, there cannot but be joy, cannot but be an inner brightness, whatever may be the outward shadows passing over us. There must be joy. The very truth of GOD dwelling in us, consciously held, ensures it, for all around GOD is joy. It is impossible we can be wholly swallowed up of sorrow while this assurance is thrilling through our being as a certain possession. As we ever and ever fall back upon the certainty, and take refuge in it, the outward oppression, whatever it be, must lose at least some portion of its distress. If the soul ever say, "All joy is gone, all light is vanished, all gladness is passed away from me,"—a soul that thus can speak must have forgotten, or cannot believe or know what it has received. The faithful soul, however cast down, however sorely troubled, will surely rather speak thus with itself: "Within me, in the midst of all this sorrow and oppression, there is a spring of fulness of joy which cannot be taken from me, cannot be destroyed, because it is my LORD." The soul thus living in faith, feeling its union with GOD, cannot but be secretly impressed and strengthened, and as this state grows into a calm, steady, continual state, a uniform and consistent consciousness, more and more of undisturbed joyousness prevails within the soul's secret depths. But only GOD Himself can sustain this state, as nothing but the consciousness of His Possession of us can be the well-spring of such joy. Its existence is a sign that the sacramental Life has become a reality within, that therefore the whole life is passing more and more into a oneness with JESUS.

(2.) Again, with this joyousness and brightness will be experienced as surely a certain sadness. For such can hardly fail to be the feeling of one who realizes the thought of the weight of Deity pressing on the feebleness of humanity; who discerns the awfulness of GOD Himself being tabernacled in the midst of all our infirmities and lurking sinfulness; feels what the contrast must be to Him; and considers, moreover, all the responsibility of such union with GOD—the risk of grieving Him, the uncertainty of falling short of His expectations, and the consequence of a possible relapse into sin. Thoughts of what it cost our LORD to win us back from sin, of what His redeeming Love claims, and of our inability to rise to what we apprehend to be

His purpose for us, will often fill us with tears, in the midst of brightest joy; a tenderness of penitence melting into the soul with the sense of its sin, not necessarily diminishing our happiness, but chastening and absorbing it, and thus making it safer for such as we are—most unworthy of the ineffable dignity—to rejoice in its security of bliss.

(3.) With this sadness there will also intermingle the sense of fear—not a shrinking fear, not a depressing, servile fear, but a profound awe, a solemn apprehension, such as weighs on one who guards a sacred Treasure for the safety of which he is responsible, or who anxiously watches a Holy Place, lest a profane step approach to desecrate it,—fear lest we should offend GOD, come so wonderfully near to us, or by any carelessness lessen what He is become to us; fear, lest we should be betrayed into some unbecoming, inconsistent act, lest an unchastened thought spring, some long-past passion revive, some sudden temptation startle us, and thus, losing our hold, our steadfastness of peaceful communion with our LORD, we sin the more fatally, because of the greater grace. Who can tell the consequences of the loss of grace in unguarded souls, in whom such a Presence has dwelt in vain? What would it be to lose, perhaps for ever, what was once All in all to us?

There are moreover, special graces which tend to further the growth of this sacramental life :—

(1.) Love to JESUS. As Love drew our LORD down from Heaven, so love opens the capacities of the soul to receive Him. Love, as no other grace, melts the inward substance of our being, which thus becomes more easily receptive of the Divine Presence, more capable of responding to the Divine call; and this love cannot fail to grow and deepen, as the sense of His love is more and more awakened.

(2.) Desire after JESUS. The desire of such a life being perfected in us, tends to its increase. GOD awaits our desires. He expects to be invited, even as He invites us. He wills to be sought even as He seeks. There is a mutual witness of His Spirit with our spirit. It is Himself alone Who first kindles our desires, but their growth depends on our cherishing, and thus, through fresh grace given, they ever more and more enlarge, craving for yet greater gifts. Daniel was blest, because he was a "man of desires." All his prophetic powers, all the grace which sustained his body in mortification, and his soul in constant intercourse with the unseen world,—which upheld him in such undaunted patience through the terrible scenes in which he bore his patient witness for GOD, preserving so pure his spiritual life amidst all the fascinating contaminations of a heathen court,—was the result of growing desires corresponding with the ever-increasing drawings of GOD within his soul. To enlarge our desires is to grow in sympathy with the Divine purpose to bless, and thus win from GOD an ever-renewed manifestation of Himself.

(3.) A third grace is the habit of contemplating the heavenly vision which has opened upon the soul, and thus feeding the illuminated consciousness, sustained by an abiding conviction wrought by enduring faith. As faith enlarges, so the vision expands. Were this vision to live within the soul, we should move to and fro through the world in its power, and life would become a sacrament, ourselves but the outward visible form of an inward spiritual grace. We should walk in brightness, in sanctity, in peace. All difficulties would become light. We should be strong to overcome hardships and adverse circumstances; for in whatever state we were, there would be the gushing forth from within us of an infinite stream of thankfulness flowing from the consciousness of the intimate Presence of GOD in the believing soul. There would be rest, because the soul had already attained the possession of Him Who is the perfect Peace, though not as yet its full enjoyment.

And surely nothing less than such a result as this, O CHRIST, O LORD GOD, didst Thou intend for us. For nothing less than this Thou didst become incarnate, and continually comest to manifest Thyself on our altars. For nothing less than this Thou broodest over us, overshadowing us with Thy Spirit of Love. For nothing less than this Thou possessest us. For this Thou hast become the centre of all true life, of all glory, of joy and peace, within our nature. O Blessed GOD, draw us to seek, to long, to aim, to grasp at, to fix ourselves on this most joyous Hope of our calling, and never let it pass away from us—no, not till Thou dost fully bless us; nor permit us ever to let Thee go till Thou, in Thy fullest gift of life, unitest us indissolubly to Thyself. Thou, in Thy infinite long-suffering, waitest to be pressed, to be constrained, even by the most unworthy, with earnest, loving pleading. O LORD GOD! do Thou fulfil this promise—not according to our own feeble desires and apprehensions, but according to the full measure of Thy own Perfect Fulness, till we become, even in this life, as thou art; that the Light that enlighteneth us, may evermore deepen within us, and grow into the perfect Day.

V.

THE LAW OF PROGRESS.

We have considered the great Gift imparted to us in the Blessed Sacrament, and its intended results; what we receive, and what through the grace thus given to us we are enabled actually to become. But we must beware of failing, through discouragement, because this blessed life is slow in its advance, because our practical state falls far short of what we have realized as the purpose of God in ordaining this great Mystery. It is impossible but that the contrast between the conceivable and the actual result should be great. And it is necessary to understand and allow for the causes of so great a contrast.

(1.) Observe what It is which we receive. In receiving our Lord we bear within us all that in our highest state of glory can ever be fulfilled in us. We receive the fulness of His Presence, all that eternity only can suffice to unfold, all the powers which will finally transform us into His own Perfect Likeness; for all grace is enclosed in the Gift which thus passes within our being. [Every time we receive, it is as though earth were transplaced by Heaven, the creature by God —God received, oneself absorbed, lost in His secret Presence within us.] We are then possessed of the Adorable Being Who fills the worlds with Glory. Or, if the expression be more just, where all human expressions equally fail, He takes us into His own Infiniteness; so that our own identity seems lost in our absorption in Him. Both modes of describing the fact are true, for equally He dwells in us, and we dwell in Him. Now, the very statement itself is enough to show, that the results of such a Gift can develop only by slow degrees. The gradualness of the unfolding of the Mystery is one essential part of the Mystery. GOD unites us with Himself, His own infinite Being, at once by a quick, sudden transport; but He wills that our growth through this newly implanted power should be according to the laws of our own nature, progressive. The law of progress characterizes all created life, and the greater the life the slower the growth. All earthly formations become matured according to this law; "first the blade, then the ear, then the full corn in the ear." From infancy to childhood, from childhood to adolescence, and so onward to manhood, grows man's offspring. Our LORD chose this law for Himself, because He would be true to the nature which He took. "He grew in wisdom as in stature." How surely must such a law apply when the transformation is not from one stage of nature to a higher stage, but from the natural to the supernatural order of being, from an earthly to a heavenly law of life in perfect harmony with GOD, and this in the case of a creature which had fallen and become almost wholly corrupt.

(2.) Consider, again, another law of grace according to which this high Mystery works. It is not intended that the Divine Gift should be sufficient in Itself to act upon us, to transform us. The mysterious Presence does not work alone. It is not simply because GOD possesses us, and dwells in us as our Life, that therefore we live in Its actual power. The difference between a latent power and its quickening into life, between the capacity for great endowments and their actual developments, is real and most important.

Illustrations of this essential distinction are to be seen in the outward material world. Music lies dormant in the instrument. Only when the chord is struck by the skilful hand does the thrilling melody flow forth. Fire is hidden under various forms of matter, which require friction, or contact with other inflammable substances, before the spark is elicited. Similarly in our nature there are hidden, stored up, vast powers which wait to be quickened into life, because they need occasions, and sympathies, and attractions to set them in motion, and only thus attain the possible development of their intended results.

There may be great gifts of genius, eloquence, power of command, unnoticed, unconsciously possessed, till an unexpected stimulus calls out the dormant energy, and then wells forth in ever-growing fulness the mighty stream of imagination, of sentiment, of power, which may become the very characteristic of the after life.

This same principle, or law of nature, operates as to highest spiritual gifts. It was exemplified in the case of Elisha. He possessed the gift of prophecy, but it could not operate during the passing disturbance of his spirit. There could be no utterance of his preternatural power, till the sound of the harp had quieted his soul, and calmed the troubled passion. Only when all within was hushed, could the Divine influence operate, and the burden of the future, the breath of the Mind of GOD, flow freely from his lips. It was according to this vital law that the great Apostle charges those who possess the assured Presence of the HOLY GHOST; "Stir up the gift of GOD which is in thee by the putting on of my hands." How often do we see persons brought into fresh circumstances—of trial, perhaps, or sorrow—exhibit a degree of grace for which we never gave them credit; men placed suddenly in difficulties and perplexities which become the occasion of developing a degree of wisdom and firmness of which they had given no sign whatever in their previous course.

(3.) The same law applies to the sacramental life. There may be an Indwelling of GOD in all Its fulness, but It waits for, It needs, circumstances favourable for its development, means to keep It alive, to stir It, so that It may come forth and pervade all our actions—as fire needs to be cherished, till the flame bursts forth, and then penetrates all materials within its reach, pervading them with its glow and warmth and brilliancy. Life thus needs conditions suited to Its exercise; only on such conditions does the mysterious Gift unfold Its precious stores. However rich, however sure Its inward virtue, It may remain no more than a dormant capacity of life, giving no sign whatever of Its greatness, not even of Its existence within.

Moreover our present state, quite irrespective of any actual sin, is adverse to any fulness of development. We must put off the body of our humiliation, and pass into an atmosphere kindred with our LORD's Indwelling Presence, the full power of the Resurrection state, before the ultimate results of His grace in us can be unfolded; and as its ultimate fulness must be delayed, so also any approximations towards it may be retarded, and for the same causes. Were it therefore merely that we abide still in the infirmities of a state originally weak, and fallen far below its original weakness; that a "corruptible," not merely a natural, "body presseth down the soul,"—sufficient cause exists to account for the marvellous fact of so great a Presence of life-giving power abiding in us with such inadequate results.

But, further, there are superadded faults hindering this development, and it most deeply concerns us to consider how far they may be remedied, for in these lies our real shame and reproach before GOD. We might have more of the blessed results of the Indwelling of GOD, though we cannot, as yet, have all His Fulness.

There may be undisciplined tempers, unrestrained impulses, irregularities of thought or action, risings of renounced evil not wholly subdued, which might long ago have been put away had we been more faithful; or there may be imaginations, dreams, visions of self, or of the world, allowed to dwell, which fill and excite us, stirring us in various ways with a constant fertility of creative power, with marvellous quickness disturbing and distracting the sensitive impulses of our nature.

Or, again, there may be hindrances from without arising from circumstances which we might escape. As outward scenes press upon the orb of sight with a bodily substantial force, irritating, oppressing it, so all occurrences act on our excitable being, and impress it, alas! so often overmaster it, carrying it away captive.

Whether, therefore, or not, the inward sacramental Presence has its true effect in us, must in part depend on the soul's own self-discipline. We need to gain the habit of self-control, a power of harmonizing our inward movements, a power like to the Prophet's harp, preparing the way for the manifestation of the Gift of God. We have received more than the Prophet's inspiration. The very Life of all life, the very Fount of light and wisdom, is given to us. We need, therefore, all the more to gain this peace, this hushed silence of the soul, that the effluence of the Divine Presence may find a correspondence of mind, a capacity for its development in the soul.

(4.) The following rules may assist towards this attainment:

One simple rule is the use of ejaculations. They tend to preserve a recollection of the greatness of the Presence Which dwells within us. It would be better with us, if we passed our days with frequent lifting up of the soul, with such words in our hearts as these—"How great a Gift I have received!" "What a weight of Deity is within my spirit!" "What a mystery of life has entered into me!" "How unspeakable His bounty, how touching His tenderness, how boundless the generosity of His love!" "The very Lord of Hosts, the very God Eternal is within me, is mine own, is become my very soul, my life!" Surely, thus, many a fall would be avoided, many a temptation mastered, many a sinful tendency more certainly overcome.

Another rule tending to the same result is to hold secret conferences with the Indwelling God. The soul may truly say to itself, "I am not alone. I have a companion, ever precious, ever dear, with me. I can speak to Him. I can take sweet counsel with Him, even with the Eternal, the Infinite, the all-perfect Love. We are one; my heart is with His heart, His heart with my heart. There is, though hidden from me, a growing of all that is within me, to unite with all that cometh forth from Him." Or we may tell Him of our troubles, ask His sympathy, implore His aid, when, within the chamber of one's soul, there is no other ear to hear. How might our thoughts thus mingle with His thoughts, our spirits with His Spirit, bearing witness one to another of what each feels!

There were once three walking in the fire, when suddenly there appeared a Fourth, and the form of the Fourth was like the SON of GOD. So it is after every Communion. At the dawning of the day I was by myself—alone. A little while, and I have knelt at the altar, and lo! Another has entered within me, and His form is the very living GOD, and we move together through the fires. The power of His Presence was on the three faithful ones; for not even the smell of fire had passed on them, neither were their clothes burnt. So may I walk with my LORD through the flames of the day's trials. They shall not touch me, neither shall the hair of my head be singed. Temptation cannot, as before, affect me; nor the evil that is around me move me as of old.

Whenever the soul is kept in this recollected state all that acts upon it acts for good—every accident becomes a Providence, every voice speaks of GOD, every passing change is as the breath of air stirring the chords of the lyre, drawing out holy desires, awakening saintly aspirations. The vision of another world is ever breaking through the expressive aspect of natural things, and we are secretly moved to the unceasing exercise of grace, because life within and around has become the utterance of GOD ever felt to be reigning within us.

As these acts of recollection become an habitual

practice, the inner being is more and more habitually influenced by it, till at last the ordinary state becomes a perpetual consciousness of the Indwelling GOD, susceptible at all moments of most blessed influences, the flowing out of the healing virtues of our LORD's sacred Body, of His Soul, of His secret Heart, working in us ceaselessly.

This most precious inner Communion is the compensation for every loss in this world, and its sweetness more than counterbalances whatever the soul has surrendered for CHRIST. It is Life given back for the life which has been left, and "life more abundantly." It is the assurance of the inward Truth of a life that cannot die, to the soul content to withdraw itself from that which is daily perishing. It is the making sure, as far as is possible at this distance from His Seat of Glory in Heaven, of His everlasting companionship. It is as near an approach as the soul can know here of the possession, the enjoyment of the Love which thrills through Heaven, and makes that higher world to be Heaven. It is Heaven begun, though veiled, secretly hiding itself till the inward sight is purged, and the will made one with GOD, and GOD become All in all to the child of His election.

Two cautions may be added lest the soul be tried by anxious fears, and sink despondingly in the apprehension that all its aims have failed, and the very purpose of its self-devotion come to nought, when yet all such sadness or doubt is utterly groundless.

(1.) The sense of our LORD's Presence is not to be looked for as an abiding consciousness, though felt to be full of blessing at the time of Communion. The blessed sense of the fulness of His unspeakable Gift may indeed swallow up all other consciousness, a power of rest and delight thrilling through all our nature. It is the elect soul's blessedness for the time; the supernatural elation which attests the invisible operation of our LORD's Presence; a sign and pledge of gracious assurance that He is indeed come according to His promise. But this assurance given, the ordinary condition of the soul will return, and the sensations awakened at Communion become only a recollection, an object of faith cherished in the memory, though, it may be, to rise up again and again as flashes of light rekindle, remembrances which still speak and say to us, "Yes, I am still here, I am with you still, though the mode of My Abiding is changed; I am thy own, and thou art Mine 'for ever.'"

Or again, there may not be even in the actual reception any feeling, any consciousness of what is received. It may be part of our intended discipline that the Gift of GOD should be wholly secret, unperceived, to be known only by faith. It may be that the soul is to learn the strength of living in the power of simple trust; to learn to be able to say, "I feel Him not, but He is mine; I hold Him within me, though I have experienced nothing; I am as I was before, unconscious of any change, yet I have received my GOD; I have not seen, but yet I believe. He has promised, and His word is true, and I can trust Him. Though in cloud and darkness, in silence and in vacancy, He has come to me." Blessed the result of such a faith, if it can endure firm and true, fond and ardent, as though it had felt and seen, as though it had all the joy, as well as all the certainty, of possession! Blessed, most blessed, if it can still continue to say, "We abide as One, Thou my LORD and Thy unworthy servant, though all is darkness; I can go nowhere, but Thou art with me; I can do, I can bear nothing, but Thou wilt guide, Thou wilt sustain me!"

(2.) Again, be not disturbed although no impressive call has come, no startling change in your destiny opened before you. The line of supernatural life may run wholly in the midst of little and lowly things.

If one sign surer than any other be chosen to mark the progress of the Divine life, it is when sanctity prevails even in the minutest points of character, and in ordinary ways. The least look, the faintest expression, the casual act, may tell more of the secret power of JESUS in the soul, than world-famed acts of self-devotion. The beauty of Holiness is shown in these finer traits, as in a picture. It is not so much the broad bold lines, the expressions of power, but the delicate touches, which impart the special charm to a work of art. The inferior workman shapes the limbs, the main features of the statue—the master hand alone can add the finer lines and details of grace, on which the likeness and characteristic beauty really depends. So, too, in our life; an occasional effort even of an ordinary holiness may accomplish great acts of sacrifice, or bear severe pressure of unwonted trial, specially if it be the subject of observation. But constant discipline in unnoticed ways, and the hidden spirit's silent unselfishness, becoming the habit of the life, give to it its true saintly beauty, and this is the result of care and lowly love in little things. Perfection is attained most readily by this constancy of religious faithfulness in all minor details of life, in the lines of duty which fill up what remains to complete the likeness to our

Lord, consecrating the daily efforts of self-forgetting love.

O wonderful Presence of my God, forgive the past in which we failed to correspond with the lavish gifts of Thy grace. Bear with us yet awhile, Longsuffering God; grant that in the time to come, whatsoever Thou willest for our probation under Thy chastening, may be cherished by us as our dearest portion—that the Inner Mystery of Thy Indwelling glory may be more and more revealed within us; and as Thou art Thyself the Gift of life to us, be also the Fulfiller in us of what we ourselves must become to co-operate with Thee. Aid us, that we on our part fail not; then, O God, most blessed will that day be when we shall stand up with the full consciousness thrilling through us of a perfected oneness with Thee face to Face, never more to be lost to our steadfast gaze, never to lose the full shining of that Light, or the moulding of that Hand, working upon and within our plastic forms the impression of Thy likeness, to be at last perfected in us when we are made One with Thee in the Glory of the Father, for ever and ever. Amen.

VI.

THE FRUIT OF LOVE.

The blessedness ensured to us in this great Sacrament of Love, as to its effects on our own inward life, through its gift of union with our Lord, has in some measure been set forth. Let us consider the effects it is intended to produce on our intercourse with others. For the Holy Eucharist is the perfect Oblation of Christ, and self is overcome in proportion as we realize what we receive of power to breathe His thoughts, and cherish His feelings, conscious of what He is to others, as to oneself.

In the prayer which immediately follows the reception of our Lord, the desire for this further grace is put into our lips; we expressly say that we offer "ourselves, our souls and bodies, to be a reasonable, holy, and lively sacrifice unto Him."[1]

This thought of self-dedication arises as the immediate result of the blessedness of receiving Christ. The soul possessed with the consciousness of its wonderful Gift, through the self-forgetting sacrifice of its Lord, is drawn to feel that the same spirit of self-oblation, the same desire of sacrifice, should reign also within us, to be the true counteraction of our natural selfishness, the cha-

[1] Communion Service. Post-Communion Prayer of Oblation.

racteristic of its new and better life; to be one with our LORD in serving others, even as He has become Life and Fulness of blessing to oneself. The partaking of this sacrificed life of CHRIST involves, as its proper result, the drawing of the heart to all whom He has united to Himself by the same bond of love in which He has bound oneself, the thankful captive of His grace.

The effect of our LORD being within us is to expand the range of our thoughts, so as to become more and more co-extensive with His own. We become, moreover, one not only with our LORD Himself, but with His whole Body. This is to be regarded as our LORD's secondary purpose for us. His first work in us is our own personal transformation. The further advance is union with Him as regards His care for others, His love by which He is equally present in them as in oneself. These two desires, (1) of our new creation in Him, and (2) of our union in love with all whom He owns in His mystical Body, breathe together in His sacred Heart, and should be felt in our hearts also, as the kindred impulses of One Spirit. The longing for perfect union with our LORD, as one's own private joy, should combine with the longing to be one with all others in whom He dwells, love ever flowing and reflowing, and gathering strength as it absorbs together into one all in whom He abides; and in proportion as this is the case, we attain more of Himself and of His Life, by loving as He loves, and becoming more truly His, because one's own heart beats with truer response to His Heart.

To see the momentous importance of this view of the Eucharistic life, we must look yet higher, even to the eternal existence of GOD, of which it is a transcript. The primal idea of the Being of GOD is that of Oneness of Substance with Plurality of Persons. There is in GOD one pervading life, one common nature, but with diversities of personality. This perfect oneness in diversity is the mystery of the Being of GOD, and is revealed to us as the object of perpetual wonder, love, and adoration. Now the perfected creature is to be formed so as to represent GOD, to reflect the Being and Attributes of GOD. He is therefore to represent this most marvellous characteristic of GOD, this oneness of nature with infinite diversities of distinct individuality. As there is in the Adorable Godhead this Trinity in Unity, this threefold distinction of Persons in Those Who are absolutely One and Co-equal, because of One common Substance and Nature, so there is to be wrought in the creatures, between themselves, that they may become the very image and reflection of GOD, an union in the midst of vast diversity of persons; and this is effected by the preservation of our separate individualities and mutual relations towards each other, while we are bound together in one mystical Body in CHRIST, as a whole and perfect Life in Itself.

This great truth has a very special manifestation in the Holy Eucharist, for through Its virtue this union of separate individuals is effected. It was because of this connection that our LORD's intercessory prayer for the union of His Disciples arose, at the very time when He instituted the Holy Communion, as the last, the crowning petition which He offered for all whom He would gather into Himself. He then prayed for the perfect unity of His elect, "that they all may be one, as Thou, FATHER, art in Me, and I in Thee, that they also may be one in Us;"[1] as "Thou and I," so "they," to be a very resemblance of the same Oneness. For this, the likeness of the Heavenly Reality, He prayed as the true embodiment of the idea which had brooded from the beginning on the Mind of GOD, as the perfection of the creature's life. And ever since that hour there has flowed forth from the Soul of CHRIST the utterance of this same desire, as the ceaseless subject both of His Intercession in Heaven, and of the Offering of Himself in the Holy Eucharist on earth.

The connexion is clear. It is as though He said,— "I have given this My Body, and this My Blood, to be unceasingly offered, and unceasingly received, as the new and perfect life of man. I have instituted this Mystery to be the same Gift to each one of My elect, Myself passing into each one in the unity of a common substance. And thus in this Divine Communion there is a mystical but most real representation of the Union of the Persons of the Blessed Godhead. As our different Personalities coalesce in our One Substance, so the different members of My mystical Body unite in a true oneness in Myself, and through Myself by the Spirit in the FATHER. I have given Myself in My Fulness to each one alike, that each may possess in his own separate individual person the same life, to bind each and all in one, even as the FATHER and I are One; one common ground of life, one substance, the same in each, yet with distinct individualities of life remaining, as there are separate Persons in the One Substance of GOD."

Our LORD, as He uttered this prayer, was manifestly looking forth over the whole expanse of the future, and embracing in His Heart all generations, and each single

---

[1] S. John xvii. 21.

individual in each generation. He was anticipating the vast, expanding, ever-growing communion of His perfected mystical Body, and so the completed manifestation of Himself in His redeeming Love, through which every separate soul finds its true relation and living connexion with every other, perfected as Himself,—the several members of the One Body become " the perfect Man," the marvellous Image in the world of creatures, of the Ineffable, adorable Triune GODHEAD.

Thus, through the Presence of our LORD, and our perfect union with Him in the Holy Eucharist, we are in union with all other blessed creatures, who are one in Him. Because of His union with them, we, too, who are one with Him, must needs be in union with them also. In Him the whole kingdom of the Incarnation exists, and in His coming and giving Himself to us, He reknits ever freshly the ties which bind us to all His elect, because their life is in Him, even as our life is in Him. The whole " multitude, which no man can number," who have passed through and in Him into other worlds, live in that common life which He imparts, and are bound to us, as we to them, by His Communion of Himself, which is the Life of all. We cannot, indeed, fully apprehend the mystery, for we are speaking of the world of spirits, and our minds are limited to the ideas of time and space, laws to which we are now subject in this natural order of being. But the conditions which determine our present nature are broken through in the miraculous Presence of our LORD in the Holy Eucharist. He is there brought close to us by a miracle which transcends the natural order, which annihilates time and space, and as we are united with Him, so also in Him we are united with all who in its power live and move and have their being after the same supernatural laws. It is said of the Blessed,—"They follow the Lamb whithersoever He goeth."[1] They, as creatures, have indeed their local place and habitation, and they cannot be present, as He is present, through His incommunicable divine prerogative, where and as He will. But wherever He is, or whatever He does, the links of their common life in Him are gathered up and knit together in Him, as the Source and Centre, the Sustainer and Nourisher, of their supernatural being, and all who receive Him meet and touch in a real communion through their common central life. There is a mystical unity, through His Presence, in an unceasing perpetual continuity of life, running as an endless golden chain, knitting all in one.

We cannot understand how these things may be, but our inner hearts are in some measure conscious of the strange reality. As we apprehend our LORD giving Himself to us through the veils of the Sacrament, we are dimly conscious of more than Himself being with us in that hour. We feel drawn to a whole world of life. An innumerable company are around us. Forms that cannot be seen are felt living, as we then live, in eternity with GOD. All we love are there. A common life, that knows no bound, is thrilling, as a vast tide with its countless waves of light, around and within us. The whole world of the Incarnation is felt in the Incarnate. The Angels and Archangels, who have yielded their delighted homage to that kingdom, who profoundly acknowledge the exaltation of a nature lower than their own to the highest Throne, one with the FATHER, who exult to minister to the Blessed in whom

[1] Rev. xiv. 4.

their LORD dwells,—they are united with Him in His Sacramental Presence. The Catholic Church has ever held that angels and archangels are around the altar at the moment of the mysterious manifestation of our LORD, and together with us adore.

And as with the Holy Angels, so with the Blessed who have been redeemed from the earth. The links that bind us to them are drawn more closely through the same Mystery, because they ever live in the same Communion, and as we receive our One LORD, our union with them is quickened afresh. We are conscious of the common life which connects us with the countless generations who are feeding on an inner vision of the Same LORD, Which fills them more and more perfectly, while we, in sacramental mystery, are being changed into the same glory.

The Holy Eucharist extends the blessed mystery of unity of life, because all things both in Heaven and in earth, are reconciled together in CHRIST, and through Its virtue all the worlds of light are fused into one. At the hour of our communion the very same life is filling us, which is filling those inner spheres of Divine glory. Love embraces and absorbs all, suffusing all whom it penetrates, passing beyond our horizon, where time and space are not, and connecting our lower world with the spheres in which the beatified rest in fulness of joy in the plenitude of His glorious Presence, even as He is hidden in the Bosom of His FATHER.

And as the Holy Eucharist thus, on one side, connects us with the multitude of the Blessed who have entered within the veil, so, on the other side, It embraces all here on earth, who belong to Him, by a true fellowship. All who here on earth live in the Communion of our One LORD, bound together in the same unity by the participation of the same Substance, are drawn one to another by the continual increase of a common love, by ever renewed outflowings of grace, and become more and more perfect in their union one with another, as with their One LORD.

The effect of this union in Him should have its practical results. Its sacred power should do away those natural impediments which separate one heart from another, through differences and contrarieties of character or position, obliterating them in the consciousness of the one life which is growing in all who feed upon the same sacred Food, and so receive into themselves the same Substance, of life. As to the eye of faith all who are His form a perfect unity, so to the heart, kindled by the same Spirit, there is one growing fulness of love, arising from the consciousness of the same Living, Life-giving Presence, reconciling and combining all together amid all varieties of individual personality, one glory possessing all alike, to form each and all, in their various measures of grace, after the same likeness of His own perfect Divine Humanity.

On this ground rests the call to active care and love towards others, according to His will Who binds all in one for the mutual interchange of loving duty and kindly services.

We rest, first, on the blessedness of one's own personal life in JESUS. Then arises the joyous sense of union with all who are one with our LORD in His glory above, and there see His Face. Then, next, is felt the consciousness of a blessed fellowship with all on earth who share the same supernatural life. The heart goes forth as it apprehends the vastness of this commu-

nity of life in our One LORD, even as He rejoices in
His life in them. And in the sense of that oneness
the heart forgets the differences which mar love, as
the mystical Body is stirred by the Divine call, the voice
of the Beloved, the pleading of the One Sacred Heart.

At the altar of JESUS we learn more and more of this
Divine Love: for when the FATHER from above looks
down on each one of us, He sees in us His beloved
SON, and in that sight of His Only-begotten taking up
His abode in us, and abiding in us,—O infinite, ineffable mercy of GOD!—He overlooks all that mars our
life, the impurities which still cling to us, the infirmities
which still beset us. He overlooks all, cleansing them
in the precious Blood, and hiding them from before His
Face in CHRIST for ever. He loves us in spite of our
unworthiness. His eye is fixed on the presence of our
LORD within us. He owns us as one with Him. He
heeds not the disorder, even though some fresh sinful
thought spring up within us. He is more ready to put
away our sin than we are to sin. He bears continually
with that constant liability to sin which still remains,
which cannot cease, except as we put off the burden of the
flesh. The yet clinging concupiscence of our deformed
nature He overlooks, as He sees the Person of His SON
abiding in us.

This is the ground of His love, and this causes our
hearts to be to Him the haven of His rest, the fulness
of His joy in us. While He beholds us as the thankful
recipients of the Indwelling Presence of His SON, clinging to It, longing more and more to be filled with It,
He has a delight in us. He sees, moreover, what we
shall be in the future consummation of His purpose for
us—sees in Its present beginnings the whole after de-

velopment through the endless ages of what His Beloved Son will be in us in the accomplished triumph of His grace. The earthen vessel is already resplendent with the heavenly treasure. The perishable Tabernacle is lost to view in the radiance of that Presence, Which the Father sees within, beneath, around, everywhere. As this our acceptance in Him is the ground of hope for ourselves, so we should be drawn to others, as He, our God, draws to Himself all who are gathered within the Kingdom of His grace; for from Him, our One Lord, flows forth the stream of life which fills by degrees all who hunger and thirst after His perfect righteousness, making all one, even as Himself and His Father are One.

We should look on others as God looks on us, because Christ is in them as He is in us. It is His Presence, alike in them and us, which forms a true spiritual relationship, and we ought so to magnify that Presence, be so lost in wonder in the consciousness of It, have such a large-hearted faith in It, that in Its power we should overlook failings, disorders, misunderstandings, naturally keeping us apart, and hindering mere natural sympathies. And if this earnest life were sustained, it would tell on all our common intercourse—there would be a considerateness, a forgivingness and forbearingness, a fellowship of kindness, ever replenished at the same sources of the hidden life, quickening all alike.

And where should this union be more perfectly fulfilled than in those who, like yourselves, are continually receiving their Lord, with such short intervals between the times of their communion,[1] whose life has but one end and one profession, of being ever most closely

---

[1] The allusion is to Daily Celebration.

united with the Fountain Head of this heavenly life, the LORD of this ever blessed Fellowship? Where can there be such an abiding, ever-growing sense of CHRIST in each and all, as in those who are knit together by the close-drawn bonds of Religious life, one in the common love of the Same LORD, and the same profession?

You would learn, were this life in GOD real and earnest in your hearts, to think less and less of differences and disagreements, to bear and forbear in the sweetness of a common blessed consciousness, so that your life would become the faithful copy of that everlasting Life in which the diversity of Persons only multiplies the common love in the One Divine Nature. The variations and distinctive individuality of the component members of the Community would but increase the harmony and joy, growing through the expression of many graces, which have their beginning and their ending in one and the same eternal source of life.

As day after day you adore and partake together of the One Bread from Heaven, so day by day you would be growing more and more into the unity of the selfsame Life, thrilling with its manifold pulsations of love, coalescing in the same centre of a common Joy.

It is often advised as one of the lesser counsels of love, for those who are estranged by variances, to kneel side by side at the Altar, that stretching out their hands together, as though closely linked in one, they may receive their GOD in personal contact, and return quickened with a common sense of the same Life within them, all causes of difference lost in the common consciousness of the same indescribable bliss. This rule should be extended as a law of life after Communion to continue as an undying impression, so that all hindrances of love, all causes of misunderstanding, or displeasure, or distaste, as they arise, may be absorbed in the sense of a perpetuated fellowship in the same supernatural life.

Cherish then this most precious bond of union, that, realizing the Presence of JESUS in yourself and in others, you may be known as His by the tenderness which flows forth from you and returns into you, the loving-kindness which assimilates you in one common unity of grace; and this not merely by a formal companionship, to be seen externally by the outward eye, but as a real inward unity acknowledged by GOD Who seeth in secret.

O GOD, our GOD, Who dwellest in that Love which purifieth all being, and sweetly bindeth together all Thy works, how blessed to hope, how full of joy to believe, that one day, if we are true, we shall enter in and partake of this same mind of love in Its fulness, to be even as Thou art, and live with Thee and Thy Elect together for ever. O may this perfectness at last be wrought in us, that love knowing no let or hindrance may draw us more and more into Thy own oneness of life, our earthly fellowship becoming a true, though faint, reflection of that heavenly society, which Thy grace has begun to form even in this vale of tears, this land of strife. Breathe it into our hearts, preserve its fervour in us. May it be the imprinting in us of Thy great Sacrifice, the power of a faith which worketh by love, in which Thou, O GOD, wilt fulfil all Thy good pleasure, the perfectness of Thy predestination in the children of Thy election, the recompense of the sufferings of CHRIST JESUS our LORD. Amen.

VII.

SPIRITUAL AND SACRAMENTAL COMMUNION.

A VERY important difference, of which all are conscious, exists between Spiritual and Sacramental Communion, between receiving our LORD simply by an act of faith, and receiving Him under the Sacramental species. They are distinct modes of receiving Him, and both are true: for that Spiritual Communion has its own special grace and blessing, has been at all times the belief of the Church, and our own Church advises it when we are hindered from Sacramental Communion.[1]

The difference between these two modes of receiving our LORD is generally understood to be as follows.

In Spiritual Communion we receive our LORD according to our own powers and fitness, according to our own measure of correspondence with His grace, and consequently with limitations and hindrances, dependent on our own defective capacity. The Gift is regulated according to the measure of what oneself is. It has therefore more the purpose of sustaining the life that is in us, than adding fresh powers or enlarging the endowments of the Divine Presence.

In Sacramental Communion, on the other hand, we receive our LORD according to His own Fulness, as He

[1] See the third Rubric in the Service for the Communion of the Sick.

is in Himself, according to His own measure of love, His own largeness of beneficence, His own power of blessing, irrespectively of our own imperfections or narrowness of capacity.

In the one case we attract our LORD, as it were, to ourselves with the drawings of which we ourselves are capable; in the other case He gives forth Himself according to His own full and absolute purpose from all Eternity of imparting Himself, in the unrestrained generosity of His love, as a King giving largesses, as a GOD filling all things with His Presence.

Spiritual Communion is as when, by opening a narrow channel of our own designing, we let in a portion of the waters of the great deep on some natural level. Sacramental Communion is as when the full ocean flood-tide rises and lifts up the waters to their highest range, and spreads itself forth, filling every cavity with its own irresistible power. Sacramentally He comes after His own way, in the Fulness of His own Purpose, in the grandeur of His own Royal Gift, and pours Himself over and within His Redeemed.

Our consciousness in the two modes of reception differs according to the difference of the Presence and of the Gift: for in Spiritual Communion we are conscious of the acting and reacting of one's own life on His Life, as we open our hearts to receive Him with the sweet sense of a love that embraces, a love that is embraced, a meeting of one's own being with His Being, in the quickening, stirring, softening grace, that the Blessed Spirit has awakened, with peace and hope renewed. Such is the consciousness in Spiritual Communion. But how vastly increased are such sensations, how immeasurably fuller is the sense of the Divine Presence in Sacramental

Communion! There all other consciousness is lost in the one absorbing sense that He has possessed us, and made us His own; that He has filled us with Himself, taken us captive, taken us into Himself, so that everything of Heaven or earth has passed into the one idea, " He is in me and I in Him." It is not merely the consciousness of being together with Him, but of being no longer one's own, no longer acting, thinking as of oneself, no longer having any distinct life, a simple yielding oneself up to be another's, because that Other has filled one with His Fulness. All other movements of life are in that moment suspended, and become as though they were not, while the soul gives itself up to the one thought, or rather,—for it is scarcely thought,—to the one absorbed sense of joy and rest, such as is experienced in raptures of silent prayer of which such Communion is the crown and perfectness, because it is not oneself, but Himself in us, Who is thus communing in us and through us with the Living GOD, Himself the perfect GOD.

Another question arises in connexion with Sacramental Communion, as to the length of time the special sacramental Gift, the Presence which possesses the soul, lasts in its Fulness. Is it so that our LORD abides in us only so long as the outer forms of the Sacrament abide in us, the special inner secret Presence received through the outward elements being lost with them? But this would be too much to identify the inward and the outward, when our LORD in His secret Gift is merely taking the outward form as a vehicle, a means of entering into us, to be with us afterwards according to His own Power, irrespective of the accidents or circumstances of the perishing creature. Or again, having once received, is it enough? Is one Communion sufficient for the whole after life? Does our LORD ever afterwards abide because of the one reception, so that after-communions add nothing to the one Gift? This, again, is inconsistent with His own word, which identifies that reception with the image of the Bread of Life, which needs to be received day by day.

How then are we to understand this mystery? A distinction needs to be observed. Our LORD's imparting Himself to us does not imply that we are always to be in the very state in which we are when we actually receive Him. This would be inconsistent with our earthly condition; it would be Heaven itself before its time, an entrance completed into that fulness of joy which is reserved as the promised beatitude of a blissful eternity, when our transformed and glorified nature will become capable of an unchanging, abiding unity of Life in GOD. It would be inconsistent, as with our earthly state, so with our earthly discipline, with the law of gradual advancement. The Eucharistic Presence is intended to be a foretaste of Heaven, a coming in, from time to time, of a most blessed accession of Divine Strength, an antepast of the Eternal Communion which will hereafter be ever full, yet ever-increasing. It is indeed, for the time, a fulness of possession, a peaceful absorbedness in the Divine Life, overshadowing and possessing our whole nature; but it is not intended that this should continue the same on our return to our habitual converse with the outer world, its claims of duty and of fellowship, its cares and its conflicts, its trials and endurances.

In every renewed reception, indeed, we receive an increase of grace, as the result of another act of complete union; but afterwards we return to our more ordinary state, ever advancing, indeed, according to the degree of our co-operation with our LORD, yet still ever, with the advance, retiring to the habitual level, even while conscious of His Presence. Not that the influence, the power of His Presence is withdrawn, but that, according to the law of our gradual growth, we subside into what we are ourselves by grace enabled to be; we return from that high converse which has, while it lasts, a consciousness of entire possession, a completeness and fulness of union, into a sense of needed effort, the exercise of our own power and energies, which, though secretly sustained by Him, are yet our own. Not that we are not still in Him, not that we have not still all the assurance of the oneness of which the Eucharist is the Divine Seal and Pledge, but that there is a withdrawal from the soul of that conscious flood-tide of grace which, pausing for a while at its height, ebbs, often quickly, drawn back into its own depths, not indeed ever far from us, not gone out from us, but hidden, its effects remaining to be worked into and out of us through active practical correspondence of our being with His, our mission in the world with His mission in us.

Here then let us stay and seek to grasp a truth to which, if we are faithful, we may ever look for renewed peace and strength. Whether we speak of the Divine Communion as receiving the Infinite into oneself, or oneself being lost in the Infinite; whether the one or the other expression most clearly defines the actual reality, we know not; for both express the mind of Holy Scripture, and are therefore both literally true. We read of being "baptised *into* CHRIST." So likewise, in a yet profounder sense, we are assimilated with CHRIST, as we feed on Him in His Eucharistic Presence. We read of being "hidden with CHRIST in GOD," as though we passed through the Divine Humanity into the Infiniteness of the Godhead, our own finiteness being taken up into the vastness and innermost Light of the Being of the Creator, through the fulness of our union with the Only Beloved SON, the express Image of the FATHER. On the other hand we have the assurance of being "filled with all the fulness of GOD," as if we contained Him, were possessing Him, as if we could circumscribe Him, even taking Him into ourselves, so as to have the whole Blessed Trinity abiding in ourselves, the outward forms of some wonderful grace, as if we were receptacles in which the ever Blessed, Glorious Godhead finds a local abode. And both these expressions meet in our prayer of "humble access," just before the critical moment of consecration and reception; for we then pray that "we may dwell *in* Him, and He *in* us."

Either way, then, we may speak of the marvellous Gift, the amazing mystery of Eucharistic Union. We may view, each oneself, as a cavity in the shore, into which the waters of the ocean pour out their fulness; or as a waif caught from a rock, and taken up into the deep waters, to be upborne upon the bosom of the great deep, moving as it moves along its boundless track.

O most marvellous Love of GOD! Thou unitest Thyself with Thine Own, and fillest them with Thyself. Wonderful and Mysterious GOD, thus most intimately near to us, and yet so profoundly hidden from us! To know Thee as Thou art, to see Thee without a cloud, without a veil between to shroud Thee from our longing gaze,—this surpasses all powers of conception. But even still more do we seem unable to comprehend Thy real Presence within us such as we are now, that Thou surely art thus in us entirely our own. This seems the more wonderful, that Eternity and Infiniteness are hidden in us even as we are. We ponder, as we seek to realize, the blessed assurance of what is ineffable, incomprehensible, what we believe and adore, as our own Life in Thee now, and long to know Thee more perfectly, as Thou art. Thou art in myself, and myself in Thee; and this in the Fulness of Thy mysterious perfections. If I return to my ordinary state, to live according to the grace given to me, separate from the actual communion with Thee, it is only because I know I may return again and again into the same consciousness, to taste again and again of the same Fulness to be poured out upon me in the ever-recurring tides of supernatural life and unmeasured richness of blessing.

The question remains to be asked by each one for himself, with increasing earnestness, " How can I live more truly according to this faith? Can I not more fitly, and with increased power, correspond with this inward Life, this great Gift of my Lord?" And, again, " What are the qualities most needful to cherish, that I may be fitted so to live in the power of this wonderful union with the Lifegiving God?" Growing reverence, more fervent love, quickened sensitiveness to the least shadow of sin, increasing care of self-discipline, more recollection of His indwelling Presence, more constant watchfulness, deeper belief in the blessed possession, more perfect guarding of all inward, as well as outward, movements and impulses of the body, which has become instinct with the Fulness of the Divine Life, greater earnestness in fulfilling the mission on which the LORD sends us forth between the intervals of our blessed intercourse with Him, the subdual of self, as it rises again and again to mar His work in us, and contest His reign within us, strong wrestling with our frailty, lest it draw us down, and cost us the utter loss of Him —these, and suchlike exercises of the spiritual life, seem specially needful to be cherished, and to be established in us.

Consider what is wanting in these respects; what is lacking in us to follow wholly the call for secret onward growth, so that the tenor of our lives may be more harmonious with our true condition, and that there may be the more faithful fulfilment of the workings of Heavenly Grace in the soul's ordinary life.

There needs, moreover, to be a very careful, constant preparation for the reception of this Great Mystery, in anticipation of the approach of our LORD, in looking forward to His renewed gifts. If we were to hear a voice telling us that at any moment we might be actually in Heaven, gazing, feeding upon GOD, in the fulness of a perfected vision, what a startling announcement it would be! What a gathering up there would be of the whole inner consciousness into that one amazing expectancy, everything else that ever before occupied us passing away from the mind! Yet what is it but the Same Object—without sight, indeed, without transference of place,—still, though unseen, veiled, yet surely the Same; the same reality of the Divine Presence, the same richness and sweetness of Divine Glory, the same in Himself, though not as yet possibly the same to us. And if so, there is need for all care in preparation, to stay our steps amid the hurried movements of our life on earth, to gain time, however inadequate the effort, to gather up our consciousness, saying within oneself, "I am going to be possessed with that Divine Presence of Him Whom I ceaselessly adore and love. He will arise and come and present Himself before me, and pour Himself forth upon me as a flood, the whole blessed Humanity of my LORD, the whole infinite Godhead of the ineffable Trinity."

And if it be necessarily so with the preparation, it must be so likewise in the after care, the carrying out practically, as we retire from the altar, of the grace we have received in the joy of our conscious possession. Even though we cannot keep this consciousness as full, as vivid as at the first, while we think and speak and act, and bear our Cross, and labour on, and go about the work of our daily life, yet the results of what has passed upon us ought to be still manifesting themselves in us, penetrating us by its power through all the expressions and outgoings of our being, giving an Eucharistic character, a tone and spirit of Divine Communion, to the least expression of our daily life. Are we not to be marked still, as we go to and fro, by signs which will manifest to all around, that the Infinite GOD has condescended to unite Himself with us in a marvellous union, to take up His abode in us?

O surely, while this assurance of the reality of His Presence within us is embraced by our thankful, rejoicing hearts, one aim, one purpose, one earnest resolution there should be to live this Sacramental Life, that we may be known by the great "cloud of witnesses" who compass us about, the watchers around the Throne of GOD,—that we are indeed taking earnest care that the manifestation of CHRIST may be found in us; that through the outer veil of our words and acts which make up our daily life, GOD's piercing eye may discern, as their vital and ever growing principle, the power of that Presence Which He condescends so wonderfully to impart.

O LORD, help us in Thy own fulness of Grace, and grant that Thou, Who art All in all to us, mayest sustain in us such a power of correspondence with Thy Love; for Thou must not only give Thyself, Thou must also give the power and the will to live unto Thee. Thou must give all that the creature's helplessness needs to keep Thee in remembrance, as we bear Thee about in us. Thou must keep down and overcome in us all that is at variance with Thy loving purpose for us. For without Thy aid I cannot hope to co-operate with Thee, however greatly I long and strive. Would that I might say with truth, resting on this Thy unfailing grace; 'It is no longer I that live, but Thou, O CHRIST, that livest in me; "and the life which I now live in the flesh I live by the faith of the SON of GOD, Who loved me, and gave Himself (not only) *for* me,"[1] but *to* me, to be *in* me, that wholly and for ever, I may be one with Thee.'

[1] Gal. ii. 20.

VIII.

THE SINLESS LIFE.

It was of old questioned in the schools of theology, whether the Son of God would have come in the flesh, if man had not sinned. Some thought that He came only as a remedy for the Fall, that His Incarnation became necessary only because sin could not otherwise be healed and overcome; that therefore we owe our glorious estate in the perfected Humanity of Christ to our lost condition. Others, on the contrary—and their opinion has prevailed,—taught that our Lord's coming was irrespective of the Fall; that it was designed from the beginning for the ultimate perfection of the creature. And it is, indeed, scarcely possible to believe that the wonderful exaltation of the creature involved in the incarnation of God, could have resulted from his Fall; that we should be gainers by our sin.

According to this view it appears that God's only true idea of Humanity is Humanity as it is in Christ; that God originally planned to form the creature on this most perfect model, that he might be raised into union with Himself; that the idea of the Divine Mind was to be carried into effect through His only-begotten Son taking upon Himself the human nature in union with His Own Divine Nature; and that this is what the Scriptures mean, when He is spoken of as "the

First-Born of every creature;" that He is the first idea, the first substantial Form of Humanity which awoke in the Mind of GOD, and that only after Him, and because of Him, and as partaking—some more, some less—of His Likeness, the predestined communion of His Elect was to be formed; that therefore it is not that CHRIST came for us and because of us, but that we were brought into being because of Him, He the express Image of the FATHER, we, in our several degrees, more or less images of Him, and, in proportion as we partake of His Likeness, partaking of His Beatitude and His Glory.

This same question affecting our Blessed LORD, affects also the Holy Eucharist. It is equally open to debate, whether this great Sacrament would have been instituted if man had not sinned. It may be said, that it was given to us only that we might be healed of the effects of the Fall, as a means by which GOD would communicate Himself to fallen man, to restore him to what he had lost. The other view is that, whether man had sinned or not, the Holy Eucharist would equally have been ordained, that through it, as communicating the life of the Incarnation, the creature might be perfected; that man, in his original unfallen condition, during his state of probation, would have received eternal life from GOD through the outward veil of this same Mystery, to be thus trained and fitted to see Him unveiled, and live in His visible Presence for ever.

The decision as regards the institution of the Holy Eucharist follows the judgment we form as to the Incarnation. If we believe that the Incarnation would have taken place as the first idea of the creature in the Mind of GOD, irrespective of sin, the Passion and sufferings being only superadded as the necessary form which the Incarnation took because of the sin of man needing atonement, so we may believe, with regard to the Holy Eucharist, that if there had been no sin, it would still have been instituted, only with different results. There would have been no healing of the fallen nature through it, for there would have been no need of healing; but there would equally have been the need of nourishment for the creature, as well as of raising the creature, and thus assimilating him to GOD. There would have been the same communion as now between GOD and man, through the medium of the same Sacrament, only no longer for cleansing, but for sustaining and perfecting the soul and body in their gradual advance to glory.

See, then, to what an exalted position this belief lifts up the Blessed Sacrament! What a field of view it opens out to us as to its real nature! For, whatever may be its cleansing, its power of atoning virtue, its first design, its leading thought, is irrespective of sin, is simply to unite us with GOD, to enfold us in a sinless Communion with Him, to make us perfectly one with Him, as it would have been before the Fall, before even the temptation to separate from Him had arisen. And still by this means, thus continued, in spite of the Fall, we are brought for a while into Communion with GOD, as if there had never been sin.

It is so with regard to our LORD Himself, as He gives Himself to us, and also in the view in which He regards us. With regard to our LORD Himself, He presents Himself to us in the Blessed Sacrament freed from the marks of the sin which He endured for us, and which marred His Beauty. His Passion is wholly finished, and the humiliation through which He is connected with sin has ceased. Though in this Sacrament He offers Himself as a Sacrifice for sin, yet He pleads it as a thing that is past. All marks of suffering are gone from Him, and nothing but the peace, and brightness, and perfect heavenliness of the glorified condition into which His Sacred Humanity is exalted, attaches to the view of His Sacramental Presence. He is there, indeed, as the One Source of Atonement, but still this aspect of the Mystery is held in subordination; it is only because He pleads what He has borne for us. His Sacramental Presence is in the radiance of the Eternal Light, in which for ever He abides as His proper Home. It is as though the storm had passed, and the perfect calm of radiant joy had succeeded; as though the restful union of His perfected Humanity in GOD only remained as the one pervading idea to dwell upon the souls of His Faithful.

In accordance with this idea, the expressions used in the Eucharistic Service in the very act of imparting Him to us, have been framed. This appears more clearly if we compare with them the mode of administering Holy Baptism. The gift of grace in Baptism is accompanied with the express mention of the need of striving against the sin which the regenerate child of GOD is sent forth to meet and overcome. He is commanded to be a "faithful soldier of CHRIST, to fight manfully against the world, the flesh, and the devil." Baptism looks to his future need in the prospect of the sore conflict against sin, in which he is to fulfil his course in the strength of GOD. It presupposes all the risk, the struggle, the constant watchfulness. But not so in imparting the Gift of the Holy Eucharist. Then the mind is led to dwell only on the Body and the Blood, which are the well-springs of the purified Life, in which we live for ever; on the remembrance that He is ours who is the Glory of the Resurrection: on the thankfulness with which we should be filled, as being at rest in GOD. No other idea is to intrude itself. Sin is withdrawn; the very thought of the possible return to sin is kept back. The idea of the necessity of having to battle with sin, is for the moment put wholly out of our view. There is no mention of it, no coupling of the miserable fact with the Presence of the Creator. The perfectness of the heavenly union is not to be disturbed. The supreme bliss is not to be clouded with the thought of our still lingering in a world of sin, of our having to fight against it. The only ideas impressed are: "The Body, the Blood, of our LORD JESUS CHRIST, preserve thy body, thy soul, unto eternal life; eat, drink, in remembrance that CHRIST died for thee, feed on Him in thy heart, be thankful." Nothing of sin, or of the struggle with the world, is heard by the ear; the heart dwells only on the thought of the blessing which has been received. It is as though Heaven were actually opened to us, and our life had passed into the Life of JESUS, into the innermost circle of the Adorable Trinity; as if the fulness and perfectness of the after-eternity of bliss had actually come before its time. The one only thought is that of our blissful Communion in GOD. All else is separated off. We have, as we return from the altar, to fight against sin as before, but at the time of Communion the consciousness is mercifully withheld, that the enjoyment of the Divine Mystery may be complete. Sin is not spoken of. It is as though it were not, as if there were no sin in us, nor evermore any sin to arise in us.

Our preparation and immediate approach is intended to cherish the same idea. The Eucharistic Service is conceived with the extremest care to put away sin, as a thing healed, before we partake of the perfect Life. We are presumed to be in entire peace with God, before we approach. If there had been sin to hinder it, a separate sacramental cleansing is ordained. The "benefit of absolution," to which the Church directs us in such case, is a distinct exercise of the absolving power, not part of the service itself. But notwithstanding this previous reconciliation with God, there is in the Service itself a very solemn confession, followed by an exercise of the absolving power, that even the lightest fault which may have been committed, even in the act of preparation, may be put away. The absolution in the Service is a special superadded provision made for us, just before we touch God, and are touched by Him, lest even the shadow of a fault, or of the thought of sin, may at the very last moment interfere with the completed joy of a perfect union with the All Holy. It is not, indeed, that this sacramental reception of our Lord is without a healing and cleansing power in itself; for this must accompany His Presence wherever He is. Such power must be specially active in the Service in which His Atoning Death is commemorated, and His Sacrifice for sin mystically renewed. But this blessed truth is, as it were, the silent undertone of the mystery—it is not the prominent idea of the Eucharist. The imparting Himself is the leading object, the offering and the cleansing are but means towards it. Sin has been already put away, and the communication of the sinless One to the cleansed soul is the one desire. He who comes to enter in sees no longer any sin to bar His perfect possession, and the FATHER sees no more even the soul itself, only His Beloved SON pervading, possessing it. It is the redeemed and purified from the earth meeting the Redeemer and Purifier from Heaven; the accepted creature from below united with the perfected Godhead from above, in an endless ineffable embrace of love.

At such a moment our hearts may go forth in an untroubled sense of unspeakable blessedness, for Heaven is indeed already ours. Our eternity of bliss is ensured in the accomplished union of the everlasting GOD and the creature of the election of His love, made one in CHRIST. This is the intended glory and rest to be enjoyed at each time of reception,—sin and the world shut out from the hallowed circle in which the soul is enwrapt in GOD; all consciousness, for the time, lost, except only the Fulness of GOD, and oneself in GOD.

Oh! marvellous gift of Love, speaking to us of the triumph of grace over sin and death, of peace in the midst of care, of the light that knows no clouding!

Each reception of this sinless power of indwelling grace is, moreover, a fresh starting-point of newness of life. Through it we may be ever more and more going on unto perfection, for it is ever a renewed commencement, both of more perfect converse with GOD, and of a truer intercourse with the creature.

First, with regard to GOD. We may start afresh from this mystical union of oneself, known and seen only in CHRIST, with CHRIST living in us to guard and keep us for Himself. If this grace were to operate according to the purpose of GOD, what would the intervals of such Divine Communion be? There would be ceaseless love in the perfectly accepted creature communing with predestinating love in the Heart of GOD; purity of the divinely cleansed soul rejoicing in its fellowship with the very Source of Holiness; peace in the soul fed by the Peace which reigns eternally in Heaven; virtue ever growing through the constant inbreathing of the Spirit's secret inspirations. Such would be the intervals of communion, if the true response of the creature met the truth of GOD; if the acting and reacting of the marvellous fellowship fulfilled its purpose and accomplished its end.

(2.) So, too, with regard to those with whom we hold converse among the creatures. As between ourselves and GOD there would be a tenderly affectionate, a perfectly trustful intercourse, founded on the consciousness of this closeness of union, so with regard to others our intercourse would be grounded on the belief, that with them we share the common lot of a perfectly accepted state of purest love,—GOD looking on them and us alike, as though they, even as ourselves, were altogether sinless in Him, seeing in us and them alike His only Beloved SON, and Him only; as though being taken up together into Heaven, we were together going forth to carry out our mission on earth, to return again and again to be enwrapt together in the Fulness of the same Ocean of Bliss. Would not such be our intercourse with others who, like ourselves, had received our LORD, if we felt alike that we were the subjects of the same amazing mystery, if the same pervading sense penetrated us, and leavened all our converse—and this a consciousness to be ever renewed as we feed continually at the same altars! How would the sweetness of the love of CHRIST animate our conversation! How would the conscience resent, and rise earnestly to condemn the very least departure from Him Who reigns within us and them, and Who had become the only acknowledged law of our life!

Some few rules for the regulation of our thoughts may be added. Dwell on the design of the perfectness of our nature as it exists in the Mind of GOD, and as it is embodied in the Divine Humanity of JESUS. Think that thou art true only as thy own life corresponds with this Divine ideal. View thyself as the canvas on which the Hand of GOD is painting the forms and beauties of what He perpetually sees in His only-begotten SON.

(2.) Look at yourself, and your appointed life, notwithstanding all faults and imperfections, as formed into a capacity to receive continual impressions of that intended perfectness embodied in the life of JESUS. Look at each one of your members, each faculty, as intended and fitted to be the organ of exhibiting some perfection of His life; yourself called into being only for this purpose, only for Him and in Him, for the one end of being formed in His Image, to be glorified together with Him in the FATHER.

(3.) Think that GOD so loved, so desired the existence of the creature, even your own life; so willed that His Own Glory should be manifested in the perfection of the creature, that after He had seen all that is most perfect in thy LORD, He shed Himself forth for the extension of the same life. He did not rest, He was not satisfied, till the perfectness of the Life of CHRIST might be formed in thyself; that His eyes might repose on thee, and say, It is " very good," seeing CHRIST formed in thee, not CHRIST in Himself alone.

(4.) Think further how the wonderful Incarnation of the Glory of GOD was marred by the Passion, His Soul desolated by the sorrows of the Agony, His Body torn on the Cross, only because this perfectness of union could not be wrought out, except through this amazing Sacrifice; because, rather than His design should fail, He, our GOD, would bear all that pain, and all that shame of humiliation; and that thus, notwithstanding all we have caused Him to endure, He looks upon us, He lives in us, as though we had never grieved Him.

O JESU, O Sacred Heart of the living GOD! Grant that we fail not now to preserve this grace; that Thou mayest evermore find rest in us, our sin being indeed wholly put away, and Thyself evermore growing unto the formation of a true likeness of Thyself within,—that Thou mayest hide Thy face away from all of evil that still involuntarily remains in us, while all the more we cling to Thee.

O wonderful love of GOD! O unspeakable pity! O grace incomprehensible! So draw us, and quicken us, that we may evermore arise to meet Thy love, that it may ever sustain us in the intervals of Communion with Thee, as we endeavour to fulfil what Thou hast purposed for us, to keep true to Thy intention in giving Thyself to us, even though temptation assail us, or frailty strive to break forth again, and nature revive to strive with GOD. Blessed GOD, this is our longing, our inmost heart's desire: do Thou accept it, and enable us to accomplish what we have resolved. And if this might be indeed our present life, to be increasingly drawn, to be hidden within the constant recollection of this Divine Communion, what will it be when Thy grace shall have accomplished its perfect work in us, and we really are for ever what now in CHRIST Thou seest us in sacramental mystery to be,—when the veil through which we see Thee now is taken away, and there is nothing, not even the shadow of any outward form, intervening between Thyself and Thy creature; when Communion with Thee will be visible, palpable, tangible, every sense rapt in the conscious possession of Thyself, and of oneself in Thee; when we shall be perfect, even as Thou, the First Begotten from the Dead, art Perfect; when we shall know as we are known, see as we are seen, and love as we are loved—when " that which is in part shall be done away," and " that which is perfect is come."[1]

[1] 1 Cor. xiii. 10.

IX.

THE SACRIFICE.

We have been dwelling on the gracious love of our Lord in giving Himself forth to us so abundantly, so freely, in the Holy Eucharist; the tender desire of union which seems to exhaust itself in the fulness of His great Gift, so far beyond all that could be conceived possible on earth. This, however, is but one, though the most amazing, aspect of the mystery which in that hour is transacted between oneself and God.

Under this one aspect of the mystery we are merely passive, receptive, only the subjects of this mysterious pouring forth of Divine Life. It concerns only what we partake of, the love of our Lord towards us. Of what we ourselves do towards Him; of the active part which we have ourselves to take, little has as yet been spoken. In love among the creatures, among ourselves, when hearts are knit together, the fulness of the joy arises not merely from the going forth of another's love to oneself, as if oneself were to be only the silent recipient of another's gift. The joy is in the mutual response, the meeting together of two streams of affection going forth from either side, acting and reacting on each other. This common action, felt to be thrilling through each other, is the cause of the complete absorbed joy; the rest experienced is in the consciousness of the sensations of a mutual affection, while each receives into himself what the other gives, and each is blessed in the giving.

So it is in this high Mystery. It is not merely that oneself receives all, being acted upon as GOD gives forth His Life to possess us, but in our going forth also of ourselves, to give ourselves to GOD in a community of loving desires and mutual satisfaction.

The leading idea pervading the whole mystery of the Eucharist, is that of self-oblation. And this, first, as it regards our LORD Himself. Our LORD's Oblation and Sacrifice of Himself is here commemorated and renewed by ever fresh pleadings. It is the same Sacrifice again and again presented before the FATHER, or rather the memorial of the One Sacrifice, and as our LORD continually gives Himself, so we as ceaselessly offer Him, His merits, His Passion, with all its atoning virtue. We offer His precious Body and His precious Blood in ever renewed memorial, as He gives them in ever living efficacy. And this offering of loving faith on our part, and this marvellous Gift of entire self-sacrifice on His part, is one great portion of the active correspondence of love, the meeting of our heart with His Heart, which constitutes the blessedness, the fulness of the emotions of that hour of Divine Communion.

There were three distinct Oblations of our LORD which are mystically renewed as we offer His atoning Sacrifice at our altars.

(1.) Our LORD delivered Himself up in the Last Supper in the upper chamber. He did so by an expressive action prefiguring His death, before He gave Himself to be received in Communion. For as He raised the sacred elements, He said, "This is My Body, which is given for you; this is My Blood which is shed for you:" and this before He gave them to be taken. It was the complete surrender of Himself, through the force of love, when as yet there was no constraint, when no violence had been laid on Him. Wicked men were afterwards to bind Him on the altar of the Cross, as the victim whom they willed to slay. But in the Upper Chamber, not even the full pressure of the FATHER's will was brought to bear on the obedient impulses of His suffering Soul, as afterwards was shown in the Agony. As yet at that last Supper He was tasting only the joy of a sweet secret intercourse with His "friends," all resting in love and peace, and the world wholly shut out from their view. But even then He consigned Himself voluntarily to the victim's death. " For the remission of sins" His Body was then " given." His " Blood of the New Testament" was then shed in will. The Sacrifice was then entire. The surrender of Himself was finished. The Lamb of GOD was sealed to death by His own free act, as these sacrificial words which interpreted His action passed His lips.

(2.) The Oblation of the Cross differed from that of the Last Supper, because it was an offering of Blood, even unto Death, the actual sacrificial stroke reaching the inmost life, and penetrating in bitterest pain all its keenest sensibilities. It was also an oblation under violent constraint, though made His own, not merely by the predestination of His own Divine Will decreeing it from all eternity, but also by His human will consenting, accepting the full weight of the Agony and the Shame, with all the aggravations that man's malice or Satanic hate could heap upon His meekly surrendered

Person. This was the crowning, the perfecting of the act of sacrifice, because an accomplishment in fact of the soul's purpose. It was still a delivering Himself up of His own free choice, though others' hands bound Him to the tree, and lifted Him up from the earth, to outward seeming, as *they* listed, but really as He Himself " had determined afore should be done."

(3.) Another Oblation was yet to follow, one which never ceases, and it differs from both the preceding ones. It takes place in Heaven Itself, before the Eternal Throne, and the Infinite Godhead thereon seated in the Radiance of the Joy into which He has entered. There, where our LORD has taken His place in His Glory at His FATHER's Side, He offers Himself, with all His merits, all the fruits of His Passion, all the virtues of His Precious Blood and the Obedience of His whole Life on Earth. He " ever liveth" presenting Himself, " making Intercession for us." It is the perfected Atonement on which the Eyes of GOD ever rest, and in which He sees His own Elect for ever accepted with His Beloved SON, as an Oblation from which pain and all earthly humiliation has passed, in which sacrifice has attained its most transcendent form of love, its most perfect union with the Life of GOD.

Now these three oblations meet, because they are mystically reproduced and renewed, in the sacramental Offering made on our altars. For, there, first, our Blessed LORD's very act, and very words of sacrifice in the Upper Chamber of the Blessed Sacrament, are repeated, and in the very same connection with the Divine Communion;—"This is My Body, Which is given *for* you; this is My Blood of the New Testament, Which is shed *for* you." They are heard again as before, and with the same results. The full application of the life-giving virtues of His surrendered life are given forth with the same fulness. For it is the very Same LORD, with the same Sacrifice and Oblation of Himself, secretly present and secretly acting as the Same true "Priest after the order of Melchizedek," through the hands and lips of His human instruments applying the same precious Blood, and pleading the merits of the same Sacrificed Body, as an act of redeeming love, separate from death.

And so, again, (2) in the same Offering on our altars there is the true representation of the very Death of the Adorable Victim; for in the bread being broken, and the wine poured out, and the Two, the Body and the Blood, severed the One from the Other, Death is mystically consummated afresh. The Eternal Lamb, as one dying, is again and again laid on the altar, and thus presented before the eyes of the FATHER, and before the world. The finished work of the precious Victim, of the one Life alone Life-giving, wholly surrendered in the Fulness of Divine Love, is renewed in a mystical Dying, a mystical Blood-shedding, and a mystical Obedience of the Will, offered through the Eternal Spirit. Our LORD undergoes a sacramental Death under the sacred outward forms mystically become one with Him, through the outward ministry of His earthly representatives whom He has commissioned for this express end.

(3.) In the same memorial Offering, perhaps even still more intimately, is represented the Oblation of the ascended and glorified LORD, His all-prevailing Intercession in Heaven, instinct with His whole collected life of sacrifice. Our offering is indeed one and the same with that heavenly Oblation, as though it were being projected from above, and extended within the sphere of this lower world, by the power of the Divine Spirit connecting the heavenly and the earthly act of Sacrifice, the heavenly and the earthly voice of Intercession. For the great Oblation in the Heavens is ceaselessly made only that its virtue may embrace the earth, and exalt the earthly kingdom of the Incarnation into union with the heavenly, effecting the consummation of His love through the union of the earthly with His own everlasting Priesthood.

Thus the three great acts of Oblation meet and live ever fresh before our eyes, in forms consecrated by His own ordinance Who is their life-giving Reality. The oblations of time unite with the offering which "ever liveth" in eternity; the earthly forms of the sanctuary without the veil, with the Invisible Truth of the One accepted Sacrifice ever present before GOD within the veil, through which alone "mercy rejoiceth against judgment." And through this union, and this alone, the lost creature is seen in the radiant glory of Divine Love, embracing and embraced. Even bound about as we are by the sin-stained bonds of our fallen nature, we can thus participate in the never-ceasing "Sacrifice, Oblation, and Satisfaction for the sins of the whole world," and know that we are accepted and beloved, redeemed and renewed, by a perfect justification through "the offering of the Body of JESUS CHRIST once for all," nay, even made "Kings and Priests" before Him, as with our hearts and our lips we join in the One all-availing Sacrifice of Love.

There is a yet further offering on our part which relates more completely to ourselves. The offering we have been considering is not of ourselves, but of Him through Whom alone whatever we offer can be accepted. It is the Offering mystically, through outward forms, of the true Lamb of GOD Himself. But having thus pleaded Him and His Sacrifice, we are then led, stirred by His Spirit, kindled by His love, to offer, as He offered Himself, our own lives, which through His Offering for us He had sanctified. It is this which completes the blessedness of the Eucharistic Mystery, and makes it no longer wholly to rest on what our LORD is and does for us. For it is not His love and self-sacrifice alone which pours forth its fulness. Our own spirit unites with His, our own heart goes forth with like impulses of love, and the joy of the Eucharist is consummated in the mutual act of self-oblation. We give ourselves to our LORD, our GOD, even as He gives Himself to us.

This is the great act which in our Liturgy succeeds the Communion, and is united with a renewed oblation of the Sacrifice of our LORD. For in the Post-Communion prayer to our "Heavenly FATHER," in which we "entirely desire His Fatherly Goodness mercifully to accept this our sacrifice of praise and thanksgiving," even the Body and Blood of CHRIST, hidden beneath the outward elements, we add an offering of ourselves; "And here we present unto Thee, O LORD, ourselves, our souls and bodies, to be a reasonable, holy, and lively sacrifice unto Thee." We thus, as far as He enables us, give even as we receive. We dare to use words which imply the very same act in which Thou, O blessed JESUS, hast glorified the FATHER, and redeemed the world; for Thou, indeed, callest us to be wholly Thine, even as Thou hast made Thyself to be wholly ours; to make an oblation of ourselves as entire, according to our measure, a sacrifice like to Thine, that the Eucharist of love may be a common act of mutual devotion; Thou in Thy Infiniteness, we in our feebleness; Thou in the generous lavishness of Thy Divine Love, we with our straitened hearts; Thou in all the glory and brightness into which in Thy Humanity Thou hast passed, we still so corrupt, so imperfect even at our best estate. And yet even this our offering Thou wilt in Thy mercy accept, regarding it as perfect in Thy sight, because Thou seest us to be only what Thou art Thyself in us, seest us only in Thyself, and lovest in us what Thy love has newly created in us, to be Thy own glory in the day of Thy power.

It is this coalescing of a twofold act, the whole self-surrender on our part with that whole self-surrender, such as man's could never be, on His part; the mutual consciousness of the reality of a love sparing nothing, which on His side gave up Heaven to bless His enemies, Himself gaining nothing, which on our side gives up only the causes of all our misery to possess Heaven, and the very GOD of Heaven, as ours, the wholly undeserved gift of freest love,—in the Holy Eucharist these offerings of GOD and His redeemed creature meet and are renewed ever more and more.

Here, too, we learn the nature and the characteristic quality of self-oblation, such as ours must seek to be, if we would be as our LORD, and unite our life with His. Our self-surrendered life will, if true, take the same course of progressive development, and embody the same manner of spirit animating its daily course. We read our lesson in the successive forms of oblation which have been already noted as marking His perfect Sacrifice, mystically renewed in the Eucharistic Service.

First, the self-surrender was without pain or struggling, out of the pure fount of a great desire, the stirring of the strongest love, while the consequences of such an act of devotion were as yet undeveloped. Such was the Oblation in the Upper Chamber of the Blessed Sacrament.

So our first act of self-surrender will be out of the pure free will of a loving heart, from the simple pressure of a great desire after GOD, not knowing what it involves, only longing to be wholly His, resolved to hold back nothing of its own, whatever the coming trial may be. This, which is the beginning of a course of self-devotion, ought to remain on throughout our whole after course. This freshness of simplest desire and trustful love is never far separate from a true sacrifice. Whatever the subsequent trial, whatever the struggle involved, whatever fearful testing may come, the freedom of this first pure devotion will ever mark the steadfast soul, the temper of mind in which trial is faithfully borne, as it becomes more and more purified and exalted.

This self-surrender assumes new forms, as did the progressive Sacrifice of our LORD, when the soul experiences the violence and constraint of the outward pressure of actual trial. Then, as GOD wills, more or less of the fierceness of the struggle, the agony and desolation, the shame and humiliation, involved in the sacrifice, appear. Clouds of fear and horror may sweep across the soul, the holy light be quenched, solitariness and the loss of all human sympathy succeed the sweetness of the first surrender, and the soul, forced in upon itself, must learn to bear alone the weight of its feebleness, the piercing of the nails, the penetrating thorns, the inmost spirit's deep wrestling, intolerable but that grace, equal to every need, ever breathes inwardly its own ghostly strength, upholding, comforting. Under such testings self-devotion becomes a deeper thing, is felt to be more a possession of the soul, matured and calm, subdued and chastened; feeding a steadier flame, though with less of the fires of the imagination; more of the will, less of the senses; more of the pure light of GOD, less of the delusive flatterings of self.

The third stage of self-oblation is like what we contemplate in our LORD now, as He intercedes for us before the FATHER's Throne in the transcendent glory of His Ascension, made perfect through suffering—like, if likeness we may dare to call it, so infinite the distance to which He has soared beyond any possible earthly attainment. It is the gift of grace, descending from above, His own precious work in His own favoured ones, which comes after trial faithfully borne, having a brightness and a peace passing all understanding, lights breaking out, ineffably tender and sweet, as from behind the cloud when the storm passes, when the soul renews its offering, as though it were its first and only real act of devotion. GOD is then felt more intimately present in the light of His love, returning after a temporary loss, because it has become more real and consoling from the fresh assurance gained through the experience of conscious support and consolations, in feelings wholly unimagined, and unimaginable, till the trial-hour is tasted —as angels ministering to JESUS when the agony of temptation ceased. This most wonderful stage of self-oblation is marked by a calmness peculiarly its own, and a gentleness which losing, it may be, something of its first fresh fervour, has gained a strength and security of peace, which is increasingly felt to be a more than superabundant recompense of any loss, and growing onwards to the perfect and abiding possession of God.

Ordinarily these three different modes of self-surrender, or such faint approximations towards them as we may attain on earth, follow each other in the same order in which they were manifest in our Blessed Lord's own life of sacrifice. They may, however, intermingle one with the other, and combine together in infinite gradations, alternating in actual experience. But the spirit of them all meet and coalesce in each single Eucharist, giving to the Oblation and Sacrifice of our Lord its practical bearing on our personal life.

Together they form the completeness of what passes in ideal purpose, however unconsciously expressed, in that mysterious action between the soul and its Lord, which awakens the thrilling response of the heart of the faithful communicant to meet His sacred Heart's love. "Lift up your hearts;" "We lift them up unto the Lord." The meeting of the two acts of love corresponding to each other, is the fulness of Eucharistic bliss—the feeling, in His Heart that He has won us, in our heart that we are won; on His part that He has gained the victory over the evil will once reigning in our nature, on ours that through the sweetness of His drawing we have renounced the evil and are wholly clinging to Himself the only Good.

Beyond this, and growing out of it, there is the further most blessed rest in the trust, to the fulfilment of which we look forward, that hereafter He will knit us to Himself with an everlasting bond of love, when the entire promise shall be accomplished, when His expectation of presenting His redeemed, in His own perfected image before the FATHER, as the triumph of His bitter Passion and long waiting of desire, will be attained, and in us the joy of an union, tasted only in its beginnings here, shall become the unchanging and endless beatitude of the enraptured soul, the recompense of a trust that failed not, through trial, at last, if not throughout, sweetly and humbly borne, His compassionate grace sustaining all our feebleness.

Let us take heed, then, that we stop not short in our view of the Holy Eucharist, as if the giving forth of love were wholly on the side of our LORD, and ours only a passive reception of His precious gift of Himself. We have an assured acceptance, as we offer in Him all His merits, all the virtues of His Sacrifice, with Himself the adorable Victim. But He looks to receive from us the response of the covenant, the resolution offered, the longing desire, the earnest vow. He accepts as His expected recompense what the heart has resolved in secret, the fulness of the sensations of love and faith pervading thankful devotion, as we draw near to receive Him, the Food and Sustenance of our souls, giving ourselves to become the Food of His longing desire to save and bless at any cost to Himself. He looks to receive from us, even though He gives all the power of the Oblation, a gift like to His own giving. His Divine Love preventing, drawing on, lays claim to all His work in us, though He receives it as if it were our own.

See, then, the lesson that remains. Before the meeting of mutual love, before the fresh covenant which the Eucharist seals with sacramental grace, resolve again and again what your special offering of that hour shall be, even as you think of what you stand in need, that you may ask some fresh gift. Even though it be no more than one resolution, He accepts it. Any mark of longing to be more perfectly His, any single aim to make the likeness to Him more complete, He will treasure in His sacred heart. Such an act must surely tend to make the life more a living sacrifice, a more entire self-oblation, and nothing less than this, O Blessed JESUS, dost Thou ask; surely nothing less can we regard as an adequate return from those to whom Thou givest so much.

O do away, Blessed JESUS, with the narrow straitening of our cold hearts. Remove from us everything which hinders the completeness of our self-surrender. O do Thou enable us to maintain that fervour with which we first gave ourselves up to the glory of Thy love! And through all our after struggles, and despondencies, and trials, do Thou maintain in us the pure simplicity of soul and oneness of purpose, which Thou wilt bless, and conform it to be like Thy own first thought of sacrifice: "Lo, I come to do Thy will, I am content to do it; yea, Thy law is within my heart." Then, indeed, we may look forward to the time in the far distance, when we shall not be ashamed at Thy coming, but shall stand in our lot in anticipation of the witness which Thou shalt give for us before the FATHER. May it be that Thou canst in that hour confess, that when Thou camest, we met Thee; when Thou gavest Thyself to us, we, too, gave ourselves and all to Thee; that we did together ofttimes seal the perfect Offering in one mutual act of common self-sacrifice.

O LORD JESUS, may such be our Eucharists, such our times of Communion, such our renewings of these acts of mystery, which, like precious jewels, stud the chain of our lives, that Thy Presence, as It increases in us, may multiply in us the graces which shall develop hereafter into the sunlit glory in which we may shine as the stars, for ever and ever. Amen.

X.

THE SACRIFICE (*continued.*)

THE act of sacrifice, as already shown, forms a material part of the Blessed Sacrament, and constitutes one great object of which they can have their full share who do not at that particular time communicate. The principle of sacrifice runs throughout the kingdom of grace, especially pervading our Blessed LORD's life. For the very Incarnation in itself was a sacrifice. It was GOD giving Himself for the world. And every action of His life in the flesh partook of this same character; for each act was a separate offering of His own perfect obedience, to be accepted of the FATHER in reparation of our disobedience, and each action had its own separate meritorious virtue and efficacy. This self-sacrificing spirit, pervading His Incarnate Life, reached its climax on the Cross when, as a victim, He offered Himself to die for us, in the shedding of His most precious Blood, for the "Blood is the Life," sealing the self-surrendered will which constituted the essence, as it was the real acceptableness, of His Sacrifice. It has been shown, moreover, that this Sacrifice of Death made but once, and never to be repeated, was not the closing of His Sacrifice. Rather it became the groundwork of a continued sacrificial act in a higher sphere of existence. He ascended to Heaven there to offer Himself for us.

Indeed, our LORD did not enter on the full exercise of His Priesthood till He ascended into Heaven.

It is necessary to consider this portion of the subject more fully.

According to the appointments of the Levitical sacrificial system, it was not the slaying of the victim that constituted the offering of atonement before GOD. The stroke of death preceded the offering, was not itself the offering; it only formed the material of the offering. It was the after-offering by the Priest of the Blood of the slain victim, that constituted the sacrifice of atonement. It was therefore as the fulfilment of the many types going before, that, His Death being accomplished, when therefore He had "somewhat to offer," our LORD, ascending with His Own Blood, offered it in the Holiest Place " to obtain eternal redemption for us." It was then only that He became, in the full exercise of His power, " a Priest for ever after the order of Melchizedek." He had been before laying up in Himself His infinite store of merit, the grounds of His acceptableness, to which every act, every movement of the will, every detail of suffering, had been adding its own virtue, and all in an accumulated fulness intensified in value beyond all possible conception, when the seal of death, in itself the perfection of self-oblation, was set upon them. Afterwards He was to commence in the highest Heavens His full High-Priestly ministry, offering Himself, for ever presenting Himself there as our Atonement, our Peace. In this "the True Lamb of GOD" differed from all the types going before prefiguring His Sacrifice. In the offering up of the victims in the Temple there was necessarily a succession of different creatures, each dying as it was laid on the altar, and consumed. One prolonged line of offerings through death was kept up by a series of successive victims; the continued succession of their perishing lives foreshadowing the one ceaseless Offering of the One Victim Who passed through death only to enter upon an unchangeable existence, there to exercise an everlasting Priesthood in the continued oblation of an imperishable Sacrifice.

The type of the old Levitical Law was most significant, wonderfully representing the inner Truth. After the victim was slain at the altar in the outer Court of the Temple, the Priest bearing in one hand his censer with a live coal from the Altar, and in the other a vessel with the blood of the victim, passed within the Holy Place; and there before the veil which shrouded from mortal sight the Presence of GOD, he sprinkled the Blood on the horns of the Altar, the incense kindled by the sacred fire at the same time rising up and spreading within the Holiest Place. Thus daily he made atonement for the sins of the people. This was the daily sacrifice of Israel. Still more solemn was the act of the High Priest, year after year, ascending further, entering even within the veil itself into the very abode of the Living GOD, and sprinkling the very Mercy-seat on which His Glory rested, as its chosen earthly abode. Alone with GOD he stood as he ministered the annually renewed act, symbolizing the perpetuated Offering of Him Who has now entered in once and for ever to abide, the Man sacrificed for men, the GOD pleading with GOD, Himself the One ceaseless Propitiation procuring endless treasures of grace through His inexhaustible merits. Through our LORD's Person thus ever presented in Heaven all acceptable prayer is offered, all sacrifices reach the Heart of GOD, sin is forgiven, grace is won, an ever fresh reconciliation is being sealed, and the kingdom of the redeemed is sustained ever increasing, ever drawing on to its perfection.

Divine Wisdom has contrived that this great act of the propitiatory Offering of the Everlasting SON OF GOD, in the glory of His Humanity, should be extended to the Earth; that we His Elect in these our earthly sanctuaries, should participate in that Heavenly Offering, and in that all-availing Intercession evermore grounded upon it. He has ordained a real presentation of the very Same Sacrifice under earthly forms by earthly hands, the Eternal Spirit bringing into a perfect unity the heavenly and the earthly, so that what is ever being done in heaven, is ever being represented also on earth. The unity is complete, for under the outward form of the visible ministry, there is the Same Person and the Same Sacrifice. For on earth under the shadow of the earthly Priest, CHRIST Himself is the true celebrant, the true consecrator; and under the shadow of the Bread and Wine, His Body and His Blood are the true Sacrifice. The earthly instruments are but shadowy forms. CHRIST is the one Priest, the one Victim, and from both the heavenly and the earthly ministration arises the same pleading, the same Intercession; the pleading of the same precious merits, the intercession of the same quenchless love. For this end as well as for the life-giving Communion of Himself, our LORD ordained the perpetuation of His sacramental act. We are to "show forth our LORD's Death till He come," and in this Memorial Offering all who are present may unite, even though they communicate not. In the case of the Priest communion is of necessity, or there would not be a true sacrifice. The Priest must eat of the Sacrifice which he offers, for the consumption is the completeness of the surrender of the sacrificed life, and therefore of the sacrifice. But this same necessity does not lie in the same way on others who are present. They only need to unite themselves with him, the celebrating priest, and in joining with him they make his offering their own, sharing with him in its blessedness.

To the soul of one thus present at the Eucharistic Sacrifice, and by faith beholding the mystical Oblation, the long series of the acts of sacrifice of the Divine Victim and its manifold details, are manifested. The love that brought Him down from heaven; the long weariness of painful toil; the aspirations of the obedient mind; the self-devotion to scorn, and shame, and pain; the surrendering Himself to those who thirsted for His blood; His night of wrestling in the Agony; His going forth to be scourged, and mocked, and spit upon, and condemned by false accusings; His bearing the shameful Cross, and letting Himself be laid upon the Altar of the Cross; the nailing of His Hands and Feet; the wrench of unutterable pain as He was lifted up on it, and, fulfilling the forms of the typical sacrifices, limb after limb laid upon it in their appointed order; the desolation of heart, the thirst, the throes, the quivering of the flesh as the bitterness of death penetrated to the inner seat of life; the Divine Humanity all wounds and humiliation hanging between heaven and earth, a spectacle to God, to angels, and to men,—all pass before his eyes; and then beyond this sacrifice of Blood, the Oblation of the same Human Body, and the same precious Blood, now wonderfully, ineffably glorified, with the same obedient will, the same perfect love, the same but evermore exalted beyond the reach of pain, the "one full, perfect, and sufficient Sacrifice, oblation, and satisfaction for the sins of the whole world," in heaven presented before the FATHER;—the whole order of the perfect Sacrifice presents itself to the mind of the worshipper at the earthly Altar, and is pleaded there in union with the ever visible Oblation in Heaven. Joining in this mystical action, we reach out our hearts and our hands together with the Sacrifice which touches both the worlds, and urge onward through all time and space the efficacy of His Atonement, the full results of His redemption, which He, the Divine Victim, wills to be dependent on such continued pleadings and intercessions.

From this its sacrificial virtue there result important distinctions between this and all other Sacraments, which it is important to note. The difference consists chiefly in three particulars. (1.) All other Sacraments have the sanctification or cleansing of the soul as their special gift, as the sole cause of their institution. Thus Baptism is limited to the one purpose of imparting the gift of regeneration. Absolution in like manner is the ministry of forgiveness and renewal to the fallen. Their virtues are limited to the benefits conveyed to their recipients. They reach the full extent of their power in their communication to each soul of their several inward graces. They minister to no further end. But it is not so in the case of the Holy Eucharist. Its objects are indeed coextensive with the whole scheme of Redemption. It is the coming of our LORD in the Flesh to be present amongst us. It is the commemoration of all the benefits of the Incarnation. It is the great act of thanksgiving for the love of GOD in reconciling and uniting us to Himself. It assimilates the Elect together in one Body, and is the means and pledge of unity. It communicates the Body and Blood of CHRIST as the food of eternal life to both the soul and body. And in addition to all these objects which it fulfils, it is the constant renewal, and so the perpetuation on earth, of all the virtues and merits of our LORD's Atonement, the continued pleading and application, with distinct covenanted promise, of His One prevailing Sacrifice. As the Incarnation involved the whole process of our redemption, even so the Holy Eucharist commemorates, pleads, and applies all its saving virtue.

(2.) Again, while other sacraments exhaust the purpose of their institution in conveying their promised graces to those who partake of them, and are limited to this end, the Eucharist on the contrary is not confined to its own operation. Wide as its own results are, it is also in a true sense the ministerial means of maintaining the efficacy of all the other sacraments, inasmuch as they depend on the merits of our LORD's Sacrifice, and the Holy Eucharist is the one only means in the sacramental system of perpetuating the merits of that Sacrifice. The Holy Eucharist thus stands essentially related to the rest of the sacraments by ministering to the continuance of their benefits. It has an universal application as regards its own manifold objects, and also as regards all other ordinances, because it is on earth the perpetual Memorial of the Offering on which sacramental grace depends. Its influence thus reaches throughout the whole sacramental system by reason of its propitiatory power, i.e., its power of pleading and bringing into operation the propitiatory virtue of our LORD's meritorious Sacrifice.

(3.) Again, all other sacraments are limited in their effects to the living. They cannot reach beyond the grave. They have their full accomplishment in the persons of those who are able to partake of them. But as our LORD's Oblation and Intercession extend to other worlds, and maintain the whole kingdom of His redeeming Love, no less wide in its bearing and intent is the offering of the Eucharist, which is the earthly counterpart of His Oblation in Heaven. The prayer in which we offer "our sacrifice of praise and thanksgiving," is expressly said to be for the "whole Church," i.e., not that limited portion of it which is on this side the veil, but also for that great and ever increasing portion of the Body of CHRIST, which has passed within, as well as for those as yet unborn, about to succeed us in the after ages. We pray through the virtue of that Offering which we present to the FATHER that "the remission of sins, and all other benefits of His Passion," i.e., whatever grace each and all of the Elect may ever need, may be vouchsafed in its fulness and perpetuated. It, therefore, reaches forth to all worlds, to the future, equally as to the past and the present. Its power of intercession is unlimited as the Love of Him Whom it pleads. Through its efficacy we can extend, as far as the ministrations of the covenanted people avail, the benefit of our LORD's atoning Death everywhere, to all who are capable of receiving it, through the power given to us in union with our LORD, as, by virtue of our sacramental agency, we set in motion and extend everywhere the healing streams of the Spirit of life flowing from the Heart of GOD.

Moreover, consider the state of mind in which we may rightly join in this great act of sacrifice. Two special features of an acceptable state I would mark.

(1.) One is love, for the whole Sacrifice of CHRIST is but the outpouring of love. His continued Offering of Himself in Heaven is but the translation of that love to a higher sphere with increased power to bless. His enabling us to make an offering which He may accept at our hands, is because of His love to us. Love must respond to love. Love alone can offer up what is of love to Love waiting to accept it. Only as we are influenced by love, which is the Spirit of the Sacrifice, can we hope to reach the Heart of GOD, before Whom that Sacrifice is pleaded. Without love there would have been no CHRIST, no Passion, no sprinkling of the Blood of Life, no Intercession in Heaven, and so without love there can be no real act of sacrifice, no union with the pleadings of Him Who offers Himself for us, no access to the Heart of GOD. "The love of GOD shed abroad in our hearts by the HOLY GHOST, Who is given unto us," is specially the grace that prepares us for Communion, and for joining in the mystical Offering. Love in its ardour, its boldness, its confidence, love in its full assurance of being one with Him in His Passion, His acts, His Sacrifice, can alone meet His love as He comes to give Himself—love no longer passive, not merely a contemplation dwelling on the sweetness of conscious union, but love actively, energetically going forth in response to His love, which, embracing GOD, embraces the whole world in GOD. In each one truly, fully joining in the great Eucharistic Service, this effect is realised. We unite in offering ourselves with Him, Who has drawn us in one body to Himself, to present us as one man in Himself to the FATHER. This common act fulfilled in the Sacramental Oblation in the Body and Blood of the Atoner, is the intensest expression of love flowing out with a power felt throughout the Heavens, carrying all before it, and anticipating the final triumph, when visibly in the heavens the Son of Man shall be glorified in His Elect, and they in Him, for evermore.

(2.) One other grace equally needful is the spirit of self-sacrifice, growing in sincerity and power more and more to resemble His with Whose Oblation we unite our own. What self-condemnation must be implied in uniting oneself with the Eucharistic Sacrifice, and with all who, whether in heaven or on earth, are pleading It before the FATHER, and yet to allow in the soul any thought or purpose alien to its spirit, to make reserves where He who spared not His life for us is pleaded as our only Hope! What a sad reproof must rest upon the heart of one who feels, "I behold and adore the Divine Victim, Who spared nothing because He loved me, Who in His Agony thought of me, and drank the bitterest dregs of the cup for me, and now offers Himself for me in heaven with all the merit of His perfect Sacrifice, but in my own soul love is straitened and self prevails." It is not, indeed, that any one can hope to say, "The sacrifice of myself is complete; I shrink from no loss, no surrender of my will; I know no swerving from the perfect Mind of GOD." This entire conformity of our being with His Being, is part of the glory which His Elect shall share with Him in the fulness of bliss in Heaven, but the ever growing tendency towards It, the keeping nothing willingly that is alien from It, the bringing more and more each part of oneself under the impression of It, into union with It—this may be ours now. The yielding up all that remains of imperfection and variance of feeling, to be conformed to the spirit of His love and self-devotion, even to the bracing of the soul to bear pain and loss, the humiliation that crucifies, the stroke that slays the reluctant flesh,—this at least we must seek to do in simplicity of faith and constancy of desire, if we would meet Him as He comes to us, if we would unite with Him as He draws us to His Sacred Heart, if we would go forth in the confidence of accepted love to fulfil the call which binds us to Him.

O Blessed JESUS, we would not take off our eyes from that Form, in the substance of our very flesh, in which Thou standest with the marks of death before the FATHER, the prints of the nails still visible upon Thee in Thy radiant glory. The Church, from the beginning, has preserved the mysterious truth, that Thy Sacrifice still continues. It rests not, saying, "Lamb of GOD that *takest*," not *hast taken*, "away the sins of the world;" and on this confidence that the ministry of love still continues, the atoning offering as fresh now in its meritorious power as at the beginning, it prays Thee to have mercy upon us; and, as we believe, so may we grow into union with that Heart that offers us in ceaseless intercession in heaven. Only grant us a portion of that same spirit, that same love, which sustains the world, and rescued us from death. So made one with Thee, may our names be graven upon Thy Hands, as Thou liftest them up before the FATHER's Eyes, that our portion may be among Thy own Elect for ever. Amen.

XI.

THE DIVINE MISSION.

It has been well said of the Blessed Sacrament, that it is at once the chief revelation of our Lord and His chief Hiding Place; the two apparently contradictory conditions coalescing in the same Mystery. The statement has a deeply practical bearing. Although in the Blessed Communion we most closely touch our Lord, and are touched by Him, feel His contact and taste of His Fulness; yet we are but perplexed if we therefore endeavour to trace more clearly His Footsteps, or think to comprehend the manner of His Presence. He is in this wonderful nearness as inscrutable as ever. It is rather as if the nearer He came, the more He imparted Himself to us in our present state, the more impervious the veil that is drawn between Him and us, as though the very excess of light rendered the vision more impalpable; the more impossible it becomes to penetrate the screen within which He conceals Himself, if we are not content to receive Him in pure unquestioning faith. Therefore it is an axiom of Truth, that while we know as a fact the reality of the Divine Presence, yet the mode in which It is fulfilled, we know not. We are at best but as children listening to some strange music, or looking upon mysterious visions, awakening deepest raptures of feeling, while they lisp solemn words, incapable of apprehending the meaning.

It may, however, help us the better to enter into the blessedness of this profound Mystery, if we observe the distinction which has to be made between GOD's Indwelling in the creatures, and His Mission. They are two distinct objects of thought, two distinct economies of grace which we can explain in words, and express in theory, however little we may be able to penetrate and understand their profoundly hidden truth. In entering into this great question, it is specially to be observed, that if we seek for more knowledge than our minds can apprehend, the vision becomes only the more perplexed, and passes from us as a dream. Obscurity arises from the very effort to see more clearly. There is a seeing by faith which is real and true. But the very fact that it is by faith only, marks a limit beyond which the illumination of the mind cannot extend. If content with simplicity of faith, the soul is imperceptibly led on into mysterious depths of an unearthly consciousness. If it would strain beyond, through natural efforts of its own power, it sinks back baffled and confused.

The Indwelling of the Divine Persons has a realization in the case of all creatures from the very fact of their creation. GOD in creating does not withhold Himself from the creature He has made. He continues to abide with what He has created, and only through such Indwelling the creature is sustained in being, and is enabled to fulfil the purposes of its creation. He abides in each creature according to its capacity, maintaining its operations and developing its intended growth. This law is essential to all created life, even in unintelligent creatures.

Divines have distinguished this Indwelling of God under three heads, which are real distinctions though they run into each other and may not always be easy to separate,—His Essence, His Presence, and His Power. These are fulfilled in His Indwelling, and in these respects He is Indwelling in all His creatures. By His Essence God underlies the being of the creatures, so as to cause them to continue in being as He at first willed each to be, abiding with them as their sustaining force. By His Presence He imparts the varying qualities and forms which characterise the several creatures. By His Power they act and exercise their faculties according to laws which are the expression of the ceaseless action of His Will. These distinctions which the science of the Saints has contrived to fix, are but the drawing out into detail of the simple Truth of the Word of God, which reveals the fact, that in Himself the Creator, all things "live and move, and have their being." The simplicity of Scriptural language unfolds into these separate ideas; for the Infiniteness of God is the going forth of His Essence to sustain the creatures, and through this putting forth of His Essence He is in a manner present, for He is present where His Essence is present, and thus His Power is also present, and has effect, and enables each creature to act and be what He wills.

This profound law of life has been in operation since the beginning, and its manifestation varies in degrees according to the nature and capacity of the individual creatures, and the Will of God for each.

But a wholly new mode of Divine communication

arose with the Incarnation of GOD. The manifestations of the SON, and the inspirations of the Spirit, which had pervaded the earlier dispensations, were but anticipative gifts, as the dawn precedes the day, heralding the wonderful Communion with GOD which was in the fulness of time to be accomplished through the links of a common nature binding GOD and Man in one body in CHRIST. This new mode of communication of the Divine Nature is called by the term, "Mission." It is therefore only in the New Testament that we read of GOD being "sent." There for the first time we are taught that "GOD so loved the world, that He *sent* His only begotten SON, that whosoever believeth in Him should not perish, but have everlasting life." And again, "This is life eternal, to know Thee, the only true GOD, and JESUS CHRIST Whom Thou hast *sent,*" as if summing up all He was to be to His Own in this term, thus expressing the completeness of the transaction which had taken place in the Heavens, in regard to the Incarnation, between Himself and His FATHER. The same term is, moreover, used as it had not been before, of the Eternal Spirit. The Spirit had been in the world of the creatures, and in man above all, in manifold active operations, striving against evil, and leading on to perfectness of life. But His special work, as One *sent*, began with the new dispensation which arose through the Incarnation. Then only do we read such words as these: "When He, the Comforter, is come, Whom I will *send* unto you from the FATHER." It was because of the change implied in this sending, that it could be said, as though He had not been present till then, "The HOLY GHOST was not yet given, because that JESUS was not yet glorified."

The term implies a going forth beyond the sphere of Godhead into lower regions of life, to raise them into some closer relations with Itself than their proper nature implied or could effect; an extending of GOD, as it were, beyond Himself to draw up nature into union with Himself. GOD is "sent" as revealing and operating what before was secret and unformed; to create afresh a new covenant of higher life in new bonds of love, as a fellow-creature might be sent amongst the creatures to represent a higher power, to communicate new gifts, to cement new bonds of earthly fellowship.

To the Second and Third Persons of the Blessed Trinity alone is this term applied; nor indeed could it be applicable to the First Person, for there was none to send Him. But it is very noticeable that a corresponding term is used in reference to the FATHER, which also appears for the first time in the New Covenant. He is there said to "come" and "abide" with His Elect. Thus our LORD says of the FATHER, as in perfect union with Himself, "If a Man love Me, he will keep My words, and My FATHER will love him, and We will come unto him, and make Our abode with him." Therefore, a change has passed over the Presence of the FATHER in His Communion with His Elect, similar to what has affected the Person of the SON and of the Spirit, some additional imparting, like to, though not identical with, Mission. A new and more intimate communication of Himself has taken place, corresponding with the Mission of the SON and of the HOLY SPIRIT.

The language of Holy Scripture has changed, because there has been a change in the Divine Dispensations. A wholly new order of communion between GOD and man has come into operation, over and above that Presence of Essence and Power, which under the earlier covenants had exhausted the relation between the two natures, except so far as the last and more perfect dispensation had a retrospective effect.

The term, "Mission," in its natural and simple sense, would mean that the person spoken of moves from place to place, or passes to some spot where he had not been before. But these ideas are manifestly inapplicable to the Divine Nature, and moreover GOD, as we have seen, had His Indwelling in the creature before the Incarnation. The term as here used implies that GOD, continuing to be present as before, is where He was, in a wholly different way, so as to produce a wholly different effect; that He gives Himself under conditions wholly new, and with a largeness of gift unknown before. He comes forth as He had never come forth before. He reveals, He communicates Himself in a way that was withheld, or could not be, till the appointed time was come, and the ordained means were provided. And the Incarnation was the immediate cause of the momentous change, the mode and channel of the superadded mystery.

Our subject leads us to confine our view more specially to the operations of the Person of the SON of GOD, since it is He Whose Presence is specially revealed and communicated in the Holy Eucharist. And His Mission is to be distinguished into three distinct processes.

There is, first, the justification of our nature, enduing it with the Righteousness of GOD, and raising it above itself to partake not merely of the perfect cleansing of sin, but of a living union with GOD. This is the groundwork of our renewed life, giving us a capacity above the order of man's natural powers, so as to be able to correspond with the grace, and follow the calls, of GOD.

The second result is the formation of the special graces which characterize the life of JESUS, and growing gradually into His likeness in act and temper and habitual tone. It is the actual impression of the very Mind of our LORD in a nature kindred with His own, as the former is the capacity of receiving such impressions.

The third result is the blessedness of conscious union, an intensity of rest and consolation in the assurance of Divine personal love, a superadded influence of the Indwelling of GOD, beyond the formation of grace and virtue, even as the sweetness and rich varied colours of the flower are a crowning glory beyond the mere formation of the fruit, and organs necessary to sustain and propagate life.

Such, generally speaking, is the Mission of the SON of GOD, acting on the personal life of His Elect. But we have here to confine our view to the special effects assured to us in the Holy Eucharist. And the distinctive characteristic of this Blessed Sacrament is that all the results of the Mission of the SON of GOD, in their greatest fulness, here meet and are combined. While other ordinances are the instruments of conveying some particular grace, the Holy Eucharist is the immediate channel of all the gifts of GOD in CHRIST. It alone contains and conveys the grace of the Divine Humanity, the living, life-giving Presence of the Incarnate GOD, and all of life that He comes to impart. The justification of our nature and person, the impression of the Mind of CHRIST, the joy shed abroad through the perfect union of love,—all are there, where He in the fulness of His communicative energy is present. All are there, because He Himself, the Source of these Divine operations, is there, in a fulness unknown to any other Dispensation, or any other Sacrament in the New Dispensation. And with our LORD, as a consequence of His Presence in the flesh, the complete gift of the Spirit, and the Communion of the everlasting FATHER, according to the full measure of His Abiding, are imparted also.

Within the range of the general results of this Divine Communion there is also a law of special grace, corresponding with special intentions. The idea of offering special intentions at the Blessed Sacrament, is grounded on the belief that He Who thus comes in His Fulness, will shed forth particular effects of His Presence in greater prominence at the particular time, to be specially impressed on the soul, in answer to special prayer. Thus the Blessed Sacrament is received at the hour of death to fortify the soul for its departure; or on ordinary occasions special grace may be sought to keep some particular resolution, or strength to meet some particular temptation. For, as our LORD is there in all Fulness of grace, so a particular desire may attract a particular form of grace. He may, in response to earnest prayer, or as crowning a special devotion, shed forth Himself in special gifts or powers, according to His will. He may assume (so to speak) special shapes of Divine life, to impart Himself, as we then more urgently need Him.

We may judge from what has been here said, what our part must be in corresponding with this wonderful approach to GOD, thus coming on His mission of love to us. It is evident that our part is to draw out, and store up in ourselves, by loving desire, and growing earnestness, more and more of the treasures of this only true life. He must be ours, not merely as a profound joy, but as an operative energy of transforming Life; as One within us putting forth His Hands to mould our plastic natures, and shape our retentive faculties in form and features of His own stature, as life communing with Life, answering the touch of the unseen Renewer of our fallen state, making us after the fashion of His own glory.

We must bear in mind, moreover, that as our LORD has a mission toward us, even so we, as a fruit and result of His mission, have our mission also to fulfil for Him. As He is sent forth from Heaven for us, so we, partaking of Him, are sent forth likewise in the very same energy of life, which descending from above is to pervade and transform the earth.

The FATHER sends the SON, the FATHER and the SON send the Eternal SPIRIT. The united force of the twofold mission acts upon us, and we too are sent. What our LORD, through the SPIRIT, hath come to be in us, we are to go and be ourselves wherever He sends us. As we retire from the Altar with the Life of GOD within us in the fulness of Its creative power, our first thought in the certainty of this blissful union with our LORD, would be to say; "I am blessed, unspeakably blessed; I have all, I am complete in my GOD. My LORD is mine, and I am His." And the eyes are raised to Heaven, moved even to tears, in the consciousness of what has been received, and become a real living possession, the whole being expanded, elated, restful, in the sense of being hushed in the bosom of the hidden

God, one's own God, conscious of the expansive power of His Infinite Love within us. If, however, in that moment of rest, and thankfulness, and joy, we pause on our way simply dwelling on what oneself hath partaken of, as though it were to end in the possession, then, indeed, there would be an utter and most grievous falling short of the Divine purpose. Our Lord's own mission would be complete, but not the mission of His Elect, of the faithful one united to Him, whom He had by His condescending love drawn to Himself, to be the representative of His Presence to the world. In that hour of supreme bliss, in which we retire from the Altar to enjoy our treasure, and to contemplate the certainty of our union with God, we must add this further thought; "He is come to me that I may go forth in Him, with Him, whithersoever He goeth. He has been sent to me, and now He sends me. He has given Himself without stint, without measure, in the entire sacrifice of Himself; and He has done this in order that in the same spirit, with the same intention, I may go forth as one sent also. According to the same Divine law of life, He is sending me forth to others."

This consciousness should be sustained throughout the interval of our Communions. Till we receive Him again, with the same renewed results, our thought should continue to be; "My mission is now to be fulfilled. Instinct with the Presence of my Lord, I am on my path of duty, in the course of which He hath sent me, bearing the cross measured to my strength. As the Father is ever sending forth His Son, so He, my Lord, is still sending me. As in His sending the Father is glorified, His purpose for which He came fulfilled, because He has given Himself to me, even so I am glorifying Him, even so in responsive love I am still giving myself to others in Him."

Bear this still in mind. So give even as thou hast received. As thou hast taken Him into thyself, so give Him forth. As thou hast been possessed by that generous mission of heavenborn love, so let all the outgoings of thy life, possessed by the same spirit, be ever giving forth out of thyself that Life from thyself. In thy acts, in thy words, in all thy appointed course, be thy mission that of one chosen by GOD, united with the life-giving LORD, living, breathing, speaking, acting after the same law with Him. What else is the fulfilment of the sacramental life issuing out of sacramental union? What else the drawing out of the thread of life, spun within thine own soul by the creative energy, which, first springing out of the FATHER's Being, has descended through the SON by the SPIRIT, to run throughout the creature whom He hath chosen to be the image of His own perfections? Such is the circle of the life of the Incarnation. The everlasting SON was sent forth that He might return to His FATHER with the gathered increase of the fruit of His Passion, and in the final dispensation, in that Day when the Kingdom of the SON shall be delivered up to the FATHER, and He returns to GOD with the full recompense of His Mission, it will be seen in the Manifestation of the sons of GOD, how much of fruit each one of His Faithful has gathered in to the Glory of His Name, in acts of sacrifice and deeds of love which He has enabled them to fulfil. The circle of life will then be complete. Take heed that the life which is thus within thee does not end in thyself. Be not as the talent laid up in a napkin and hidden in the earth, profitless, the possession of the slothful, the doom of the unfaithful. Rather go forth with it that it may bear fruit, that thy "LORD, at His coming, may receive His own with usury;" that He may then see the faithful development of His Life in thy own person, "chosen of GOD and precious," as He gave up His own Divine Person for thee. And as we cannot penetrate the manner of the Presence of this Life within us, though we experience its workings, so in your case others will feel the effect of the Presence of GOD with thee, will see that thou "hast been with JESUS," while yet the secret cause, the inner Life Itself working in thy inner being, they will have no sense to apprehend, so inscrutable is that mystery, of which thou art the subject, which yet ever more and more manifests itself through thy outward form.

O Blessed JESUS, do Thou grant that as we are indeed Thine own, in whom Thou willest thus to communicate the fulness of Thy gifts, so we may not faint or sink beneath the burden of Thy Divine Nature thus wonderfully infused into us, nor disappoint Thy expectations; but may continue pressing forward towards the end, the prize of our high calling, in earnest endurance and careful self-discipline, that so we may be known as Thine, and Thou mayest be glorified in us.

O hidden GOD! hidden even from ourselves, more and more hidden, as we approach ever nearer and nearer to Thee, grant that Thy inscrutable Presence may at last shine forth in us in all the glory of Thy Divine life, which Thou hast willed us to attain, that meanwhile its fruit may abound, and we become the blessed instruments of Thy will, the manifestations of Thy Mind, in our day, even as Thou hast ordained for us. Amen.

XII.

THE RETREAT ON THE MOUNT.

The time of Holy Communion is a Retreat, a solitude in the immediate Presence of God even though we may be in the midst of a crowd. It resembles the scene upon the Mount, where Moses met God, and the Lord passing by revealed Himself. Moses was alone with God, retired from the world, raised above it, and above all intercourse with external objects, in the stillness which reigns on mountain summits, a faint image of the ineffable peace which surrounds the Home where the Redeemed will at last find their rest in God. Holy Communion is the covenanted anticipation of that peace.

Moses was called by God Himself to enter into his Retreat, in order to bring his mind into harmony with the Revelation he was about to receive.[1] For care and anxiety had brooded heavily on his mind, oppressed with the burden of the sins of the people whom he was leading. He had trembled at the prospect of the possible withdrawal of God's Presence and support, and his own failing from conscious helplessness. In this troubled state he sought peace; and what was his resource? It was not enough for him that the Angel's Presence was assured to him. It was not enough that the sins of his people or his own failings of heart should be forgiven;

[1] Exod. xxviii.

not enough that the Covenant of peace was renewed. There arose within his soul an intense desire soaring far beyond all these assurances, the desire for light and guidance from a personal manifestation of GOD Himself. And this desire could not rest without an earnest effort to gratify it. From the profound longing arose the intense cry: "I beseech Thee, show me Thy Glory." All lesser influences passed from his soul, even fear, and the burden of care, and the sense of loneliness. All supports of a subordinate kind, the rich promises, the prophecies, and the many external signs of the nearness and unfailing Almighty power of GOD, sank into comparative insignificance. His soul had risen to the apprehension of a Vision of blessedness beyond all that had as yet been vouchsafed to him. The merciful answers to his previous prayers had encouraged him to ask for what alone could satisfy him now, and leave behind no possibility of doubt or fear for ever afterwards. "Show me Thy Glory." Unveil Thyself. Remove this screen, this thick cloud that gathers round Thee, notwithstanding Thou art ever near to me. However closely my soul feels Thy Presence, it is not enough; let me see Thee. Reveal the mighty secret of Thy Nature. Show me Thyself.

Observe how wonderfully GOD meets this desire. A response far beyond what Moses could possibly have realized, though so far less than he had dared to ask, breaks forth from the cloud. Out of the depths of the Being of GOD a Voice spoke—"I will make all My Goodness pass before thee." I will indeed proclaim My Name, and thou shalt know Me in all My Love. The words seem to imply that GOD had been waiting for an opportunity to reveal Himself to His servant, as if in the fulness of His own desire, He was taking advantage of His servant's prayer. There is no pause, no hesitation in meeting the request so far as it could be granted. When afterwards GOD fixes a limit to His revelation of Himself, it does not appear as though He were unwilling to grant even the full desire, that there was any hindrance in Himself, but only because His servant was unable to endure the Brightness of the Vision. "Thou canst not see My Face." It is not that He would withhold anything that had been asked. In the Divine Mind Itself there is no apparent reluctance. "Thou canst not." It is the incapacity of the Creature, not the reserve of GOD. The hindrance arises partly from the necessary limitation of a created nature, partly from the consequences of the Fall,—not from the alienation of the Divine Nature. That "No man can see GOD and live," expresses a law that affects the conditions of created life, not the Creator's love. And in what follows we see how with most studious care GOD, in granting His servant's desire, guards him against the possible risk even of the Revelation which he was capable of receiving, tempering the intensity of the splendour of the communication by the interposing veil within which He withdraws, as He reveals, Himself. GOD places Moses "in the cleft of a rock," and with His own Hand covers him as He passes by, so that His servant may see the lingering radiance that hung around His retiring Form, when it was impossible for him to behold the Face or Substance of His Presence. The fact, however, remains, that the Glory of GOD which he asked to see, did pass by him with no veil save the covering of His Own Hand, an outshining of His Own Person between Himself and His servant's eyes. It was not, however, as we learn from the words in which GOD expresses Himself, His Own Person in His very Essence, on Which Moses thus looked through this veil, but only His moral Glory, His Mind, His essential character, His "Goodness," the ineffable perfection of the attributes of His secret Heart.

What Moses actually saw in that hour, he saw as a reflection in his own being. It was not that which was external to himself that he was looking upon, but by an introspective gaze he saw that external object which passed by, cast upon the spectrum of his own soul, as in the bodily sight the eye does not see the object itself, but its reflection in its retina, an object within itself which is the counterpart of the real object on which the eye gazes. The great Prophet, in the hour of his marvellous contemplation, saw within the glass of his own being the Image, the representation of the inner Mind of GOD Himself. It was to him as it will be at the last great day when GOD Himself, the One Object absorbing all other objects, will form a reflected vision of Himself within the souls of the redeemed, and in the glorious contemplation of that inner world, the veil being at last withdrawn, there will be a twofold Vision,—the very Person of GOD Himself consciously apprehended, and His Form of glory reflected within to be the possession of the soul itself. For thus the scriptural expression which speaks of the Vision is to be understood, "Face to face," Object to object; the Glory displayed so as to be apprehended within by all who are capable of receiving Him; the objective and the subjective Visions become one, coalescing and embracing each other, to be ever developing into profounder depths of consciousness through the endless ages.

This Vision will not be as the passing shadows which occupy our sight here on earth; for the glorious Form reflected in the soul to which the Face of GOD is revealed, is an actual real Presence in the soul, and is there not merely by a reflective faculty, or by the introspective gaze of the soul looking into itself, but as an abiding power which diffuses itself within the substance of our being, which stamps itself upon us as upon a seal, penetrates it, conforms it to itself, takes it up into itself, till the soul becomes the very Life of GOD, a life therein revealed, not merely as an image reflected in a glass which when a man passes by he sees no more, because the object reflected is no more within the scope of his vision, and was there only because he gazed upon it, his eye itself creating it for his momentary embrace as a fleeting thought,—but as a life which abides, as a distinct form of character, as a very shape and substance which the receptive faculties of the ever-gazing soul absorb within, entranced, transubstantiated into it. This glory, this blessed seal of the living GOD, this inward vision, which is the reflection of the vision which the illuminated spirit by faith beholds, grows in its measure in this present state, and is the ground of the inner sacramental life.

The full glory of the Divine Communion is, that the very substantial Presence of the Living GOD is communicated, and the soul receives and feeds on the very Light and Power of the Vision which in faith it beholds, to be formed after its Likeness. The two, the Vision and the new character of life formed after It, are the result of the Divine Communion, the new creation of GOD in the soul of His Elect, which, as He passes by, He casts from Himself as the reflected glory of His veiled Presence, to be an abiding possession.

Each return to the Blessed Sacrament is the re-entering into a Retreat in which such a life is again and again renewed. It is going where the LORD is to be seen more ready to reveal Himself than we to ask the grace which He reveals; a fresh gazing on His Goodness which He spreads out before us, that He may conform to Himself the inner life as it receives the impression, and pledges itself with renewed fervour to rise to that supernatural union with Him, which is the true fulfilment of His purpose for us.

Viewing, then, our Eucharistic Communion under this aspect in harmony with this scene upon the Mount, let us lay to heart some lessons which may be helpful to us, in order to correspond more perfectly with the intention of GOD.

I would not dwell on the abstraction of thought which is manifestly needed to divest the soul of care and anxiety, the quietness that should reign around one's life that it may be separated from outward things, so as to place the soul in the attitude most truly in unison with GOD's revelation of Himself. This absorbed recollectedness is a self-evident condition of such seeking after GOD; but besides this there are special points taught in this scene, which may be less apparent.

(1.) In the largeness of desire expressed in the prayer of Moses there is a lesson as well as an encouragement. It teaches us that we may be bold with GOD. It implies that GOD is generous, and that we may presume on His generosity; that we may draw largely upon His Benignity. We may take for granted His willingness to be lavish in His gifts. There is too often an absence of this trustful spirit even in the holiest persons, the most surely accepted worshippers of GOD. There is a trembling fear lest one feeling himself unworthy should ask too much, lest the petition should be beyond the possible gift of GOD. Or there is a misgiving as to the possible consequences of aspiring for any high revelation of GOD, as if the soul were incapable of corresponding with it. Mingled with this there is, moreover, the influence of old habits, of prepossessions marring the soul's expanding energies, and preventing the onward pressure of grace. Further there is the fear of risk, where there may have been failing before,—risk lest the soul should draw down upon itself a judgment because of renewed failure, rather than an increase of grace because of renewed desire.

We see no trace of such feelings of apprehension in the case we have contemplated. On the contrary, there is courage and confidence, the utmost possible reaching forth of the soul breaking beyond all bounds of past experience. We see a grand scope of fervent desire rising up so as to embrace the very fulness of the bliss of heaven, even though the soul which breathes such a desire had been just before weighed down with the utmost fear and anxiety. Surely when GOD responded to this desire He meant to show that He was pleased with it, that He would deal, as He had been dealt with, generously; that He would reveal Himself largely to a largeness of heart resembling His own.

(2.) We learn, that when GOD answers such desires, He is careful that what we ask shall only be given so far as is safe for us. As He placed His Hand between Moses and His unveiled Glory, allowing His servant to look only on what he could endure, even so surely will He guard us against the risk that attends any rashness in the longing, while He grants the utmost fulness of desire that He approves, giving what we are able to receive, while He withholds what would only injure us. Therefore even in making large requests and fresh resolutions, we ought to be always trustful, that He will limit the meaning of our petition to the capacities which He recognises in our souls. He will acknowledge the truth of our intention, even though our words may be beyond our power, and accept us according to what He knows our spiritual capacity to be.

(3.) Again, with this largeness of desire there must be the growing readiness to correspond with the grace that the desire wins, a will to embrace the revelation of GOD in its practical results. Moses was evidently advancing in the consciousness of an increasing capacity while on the Mount. At first his mind appeared only to take in the need of the guiding and supporting Presence of GOD, to sustain him in his onward course under so great a pressure. But his soul grew in its hopes of attainment, and at last he rose up to the idea of apprehending the full greatness of the Mind and Character of GOD. This growth of the human mind, when fixed earnestly on any definite aim, is one of its most important laws. A mind really giving itself to acquire any particular science, grows rapidly in the power of apprehending fresh deepening views as they open in its pursuit. As an advance is made in knowledge the mind is enlarged and strengthened in its capabilities of receiving more truth. Both the field of knowledge enlarges, and the mind increases in power of intelligence; and with the power the appetite or desire to increase enlarges also. This law of the growth of the mind in natural science, is analogous to the growth of the soul fixed upon GOD, in the longing desire to apprehend Divine truth. The vision of GOD grows with the desire to apprehend Him, and both the capacity and desire of the soul increase with the enlarging vision; they act and react upon each other. And the growth will continue according to this law of mutually responsive action, a growing vision of GOD, and an ever-growing desire of the faithful soul, each attracting the other, each developing with the other, till they become one in an infinite capacity, so that the creature knows even as it is known.

(4.) Again, this same intercourse of the great Saint of the Old Covenant with GOD, explains a fact at which men often marvel. How wonderful it is that while so much is hidden from us, we are yet enabled to see so much! Both the hiding of the Hand of GOD, and His revealing, are alike wonderful. His Hand is placed before our eyes to conceal, when yet we see as through the cleft secret depths of His inmost Heart, which even Angels desire in vain to look into. While an impenetrable veil is spread before our sight, yet what startling openings, what unexpected glimpses of that world of life, of the mystery of the Presence of GOD, are at times mercifully vouchsafed to us! And we are, in truth, sensibly drawn on by this alternation of the two apparently irreconcilable principles of concealment and revelation.

(5.) Again, we here learn to lay to heart how good it is to wait upon the LORD, to watch the opening Vision with minds calmly set to abide His time, and though with growing desire to understand, yet acknowledging our unworthiness to apprehend, our incapacity of judging what knowledge may be good for us, what may be hurtful. There are times and seasons for the revelations of GOD, ebbs and flows of His movements, and He Who knows what is in man, can alone judge when we can see and live. There may often be the greater blessing in the expectancy, in the resolution to wait, to acknowledge our ignorance and trust, and so abide peacefully in the cleft of the Rock, confident that when He lifts the veil before our purged sight, we shall find that the time of probation for such wondrous bliss was most surely needed. The greatest marvel at last will be, that to such as we have been, the light was ever vouchsafed, and that yet an eternity lies beyond, incapable of exhausting the wonders of the Vision.

(6.) We must keep in mind the difference between ourselves and the Prophet of the earlier Covenant,— a difference which raises us incomparably above his condition, so that the Vision which only "passed by him," is for us an ever-renewed Presence, even our LORD Himself, because He is come to abide in us, and is ever revealing Himself to the illuminated soul which has faith to embrace Him. He reveals Himself not only for a moment when His servant is called up to the Mount, as one incident in his mysterious journey; we can enter as we will into Retreat with Him within our own hearts, uniting ourselves with Him by the abiding power of a living faith, which is "the substance of things hoped for," the unfailing "evidence of things not seen." We are ever standing on the Rock. We are ever being touched by the Glory which is passing by. We are ever seeing through that

Hand whether It conceal or open the Vision. Only we must preserve our soul's capacity thus to apprehend by diligent care and watchfulness, lest the world draw us down, and thus narrow our capacity for GOD, or debase our spiritual taste, or chill the ardour of our desires. We must bear in mind that with the ever-renewed and increasing revelation, there must be a growing conformity with the Vision as It is revealed to the eyes of faith, an actual working out of its results in the visible life, according to the law which ever accompanies the promise; "The just shall live by his faith."

O LORD, unless Thou Thyself Who art the unspeakable Gift, be also the Giver of the grace to receive the Gift, how shall we be sufficient for these things? In the lavishness of Thy outpoured love prepare Thy servants, that with inspired spirits they may apprehend the heavenly Vision; that nothing may be lost of that which Thou art gone to prepare for them; that their after life may bear witness to the blessings which Thou hast shed upon them, through Him Who is the only "Light that lighteneth every man that cometh into the world," to Whom be glory for ever.

XIII.

THE REPOSE OF FAITH.

The life of sacramental union with God seems strange and alien to our natural life, and impossible to reconcile with our sinfulness and many infirmities. That this apparent contrariety, however, is no evidence of its unreality may be concluded from the amazing contrast which exists between our Lord and the poor earthly elements through which He condescends to communicate Himself. He speaks as though He recognized no difference between those earthly elements and Himself. He speaks of Himself and them as one—"This is My Body;" "This is My Blood." The words imply a sacramental identity; and where His Body and His Blood are, there by virtue of the Hypostatic Union is Christ Himself.

If it were an angelic presence to be thus associated with forms of earth, the contact would seem to be impossible. Were such a Presence revealed it would be more than our nature could bear; for when, as we read in the Old Testament, angels appeared, though veiled under kindred human forms, the sight was so overpowering that even prophets beholding them were as men struck dead.

No marvel, therefore, that the contrast involved in a sacramental union, not with an angel or archangel, but with the Creator of angels, with the Everlasting God Himself, must appear a thing impossible. If one could not see His Face and live, how can we actually receive Him within our nature, and not be overwhelmed? How go forth, and not sink beneath the weight of such a Presence? But if the poor earthly elements preserve their being in such a marvellous union; if such a reconciling of the Uncreated and created is possible; if He can condescend to such a position relative to the inanimate creatures, the argument against our possible union with Him, because of the infinite contrariety of nature, the contrast of His greatness and our nothingness, falls to the ground.

It is but one part of the mystery, that God has so accommodated Himself to our capacities, so restrained His communication of Himself, that we feel not His real greatness. He so tempers His approach, so veils His Majesty, that the Divine Communion becomes the gentlest, the tenderest, the most perfectly restful hour of our life. As we advance in spirituality, and so come nearer to God, this profound mystery will not appear less strange than it did at first. On the contrary, as our eyes become more purged to see, as our spiritual power becomes greater, so the more incomprehensible is the truth. Hereafter, when we shall have passed where all is light, and we behold the mystery in the full radiance of the glory of the world to come, it will strike us with yet greater amazement, that such an accommodation of the Infinite Godhead to our littleness could have been made possible even to infinite Love.

There is, indeed, nothing to which we can compare it. Nowhere throughout the creation has God communicated Himself in such fulness as to His own Elect. The

Hypostatic Union, the union of the Divinity with the Humanity in CHRIST, is the one only example with which we can compare our new state. Among the creatures the transformation we are contemplating stands absolutely alone. Next to GOD Himself, and inferior to Him alone, we stand in the order of the creation, yet essentially separated from it by this distinction. It is not merely that He is in us, as the Author of our Being, as He stands related to the inanimate creatures, or as the Author of life to living creatures, or as the Author and Preserver of the powers of sensation to sensible creatures, or as the Author and Revealer of knowledge to intelligent creatures, nor merely as the Sustainer of supernatural powers of life, as He is the Fulness of a supernatural glory to the angels and Heavenly Hierarchies. Above and beyond all this, through the communication not merely of powers and gifts, but of Himself, and through impressing the very Likeness of Himself in a nature akin to His own, He stands related to us; and this not by one act, one exercise of love, but by an ever renewed imparting, like to the pulsations of the ceaseless flow of light which in the material world gladdens and glorifies nature, by His own Infinite attributes adapting themselves in a special and most marvellous manner, a very oneness of life, through the actual Presence of Himself, the Very Substance of the Very GOD.

It is to be noted that the communications of this Divine Life act primarily and directly on the spirit, or higher element of our nature. What S. Paul says of the HOLY GHOST, "The Spirit witnesseth with our spirit," is true also of the Divine Humanity and the Presence of CHRIST in us. It is with the spirit, or highest faculty of our complex nature, that He holds His mysterious intercourse, coming first into contact with it, and there first imparting Himself.

He Who, though in a true human Body, the very same Body that He took of His Virgin Mother, and in which He hung on the Cross, is yet all Spirit, first seeks that in us which is most nearly kindred with the spiritual Body in Which He now abides in Heaven with the FATHER. From thence, from His first high converse with the spirit within us, His Presence descends, as it were, to the lower component parts of our nature, taking up into Itself, or diffusing Itself into, all our faculties and organs in order, by a mysterious accommodation of Himself passing throughout even our material structure, our very bones and flesh, making our bodies a temple for Himself. His own Body and His own Blood glorified, resplendent with the light of Deity, find even in our natural bodies a home, a means of communication and of abiding, so as to hold intercourse with us, and impress Himself upon us even unto the extremities of our being. How strange it is, that even the higher portions of our being can be sustained in communion with the Eternal Spirit! How much more strange that any lower or more ordinary faculty can be brought into contact with such a communication of Himself!

And yet what a contradiction to Himself must He experience; what a revulsion to His own Divine consciousness, when He enters within us! It is as though a foreigner were to arrive in some distant land, and find there habits and customs, tastes and associations, wholly different from what he had known in his own land, a different language, and unwonted means of support.

Such is our Lord's coming to us. Too truly still "His ways are not our ways, neither His thoughts our thoughts." The Invisible, the All Perfect, the Holy One, God from out of the depths of His own Land of Glory, coming and raising His tabernacle in the midst of our fallen nature, seems strange to the one in whom He comes to make His abode. He comes as a wayfaring man among a people of a strange tongue, scarcely finding means of communication or common ideas. Only by degrees the powers of intercourse and capacity of understanding grow up. Slowly He is able to communicate Himself as He desires. Slowly we are able to understand Him. Yet just as the traveller, tarrying patiently in his new abode, finds more and more kindred ideas hidden beneath the apparent differences, and grounds of mutual trust, so that at last where all had been so strange, he finds a second home, his cravings for sympathy and companionship satisfied, even so our Lord finds by degrees, or rather creates within us for His own rest in us, capacities to understand Him, and inclinations, one with His own, thoughts and tastes in common; and we, too, become conscious of seeing Him no longer as a stranger and sojourner, and apprehend His meaning, and know His voice, and correspond with His movements. And then more and more consciously is felt a power of intercourse, the interchange of thoughts and ideas; and what was once so contradictory becomes clear, and full of a wonderful delight, a joy of fellowship, a rest of trustful, mutual love, though with increasing amazement and even with growing fear, because the more we understand Him, so much the more the awfulness of His Majesty, and the sanctity of His Presence, come forth to view, brood over us, and haunt us with a power before which gradually other consciousness fades, other intercourse becomes comparatively as of no account,—all else seen to be of the earth, earthy, and this, the Second Man, the LORD from Heaven, the true and only Life.

Most important it is to understand what it is that has to be brought about, before this Union, however firmly sealed in Sacraments, will become to us an actual and conscious reality.

Two ends have to be gained. One is to naturalize (if we may use the expression) in our souls that mysterious union of our LORD with our own hidden inner life, to adjust the two lives, harmonizing the play of both powers, to form our own ideas into sympathy with His, to turn all our desires into the same current of feeling in which His desires find their rest, to " bring," as S. Paul expresses it, "every thought into the obedience of CHRIST," into obedience to that strange Presence which has possessed us, that thus He, our GOD, may become the reigning, all-directing LORD and King of His new, His chosen abode.

Secondly, we have to naturalize ourselves to the new world which has grown up around us as strange to us, as His Presence was strange at first. For all has changed, even as we ourselves have changed, with the new life which has possessed us. Where He is, Heaven must soon unveil itself. All that is visible, or tangible, assumes a new colouring. "Old things are passed away, behold, all things are become new."[1] As we become consciously possessed with that new Life, and our whole nature grows into harmony with It, so necessarily we look on outward nature, on those with whom we have

[1] 2 Cor. v. 17.

to do, on the events and passing incidents with which we are brought in contact, with different eyes, viewing them in new relations, with a new sense of duty and a higher love, interpreting them now according to the Mind of GOD, seeing them as He sees them, thinking of them, dealing with them, feeling towards them, as in GOD, as we bear about His Presence within us. At first, indeed, as our new life opened to us, all these outward objects—even those most dear to us, even those most closely and most commonly associated with us—seemed no longer in harmony with us as before. We know not at first how to reconcile the newly-acquired consciousness with the old relations, how to adjust the claims of the new life and those of the natural life still so closely bound about us. We feel at first as if by what seems a translation into a new order of being, we had become aliens to our former friends and companions; we fear to lose our new-found treasure if we continue our wonted intercourse with those to whom nature's fond ties had linked us; we see not how we can continue true to the one without being false to the other; we are perplexed and anxious. It requires time to see truly, as changed objects require a change of focus in the instrument of vision. Only by degrees do we see how we may become really more true to the one life, as we become true to the other; that the new point of vision and the new consciousness in GOD, have not really necessarily separated us from our former ties, rather have brought us closer together in Him; have not removed us further, only translated both together into a higher sphere of being. What was dear before has become yet dearer in CHRIST, Who now rules our hearts. What claimed of us duty or love after the natural order, has laid on us the sweet pressure of a higher love, a more exalted dutifulness. All has risen to a higher perfection, but nothing is really lost within the changed field of view, as the eye more and more acquires the delighted power of seeing all in their true relative positions, each receiving a fresh meaning and a deepened interest by the new connexions which have been formed. The purged spirit, taught to gaze on the supernatural life within, around it, sees more truly what nature claims of God, how the will of the Lord is fulfilled in all that bears the stamp of His own ordaining. Nature and Grace become one in Him Who is the Author and Preserver of both the worlds, or rather Who makes the one the instrument of developing the other, as the Resurrection body rises out of the body of our humiliation.

There are four practices that may be mentioned as helpful to the attainment of this state of spiritual understanding.

(1.) One is an introspective Communion with what is going on in us, meditation on the mysterious facts on which we have dwelt, and their issues; the communing within, the conference held in wondering adoring love with the august Truth, of what nevertheless no sense, however fine or delicate, can appreciate or take cognizance. Moreover, beside this inward musing on the mysterious certainty, the exercise of the enkindled imagination on what it involves, what it demands, its laws, its habits, its inspirations, its faint whisperings, its gentle impulses of all that is " pure and lovely and of good report," there arises the thought, how to fulfil, how to apply these high instincts, these heavenly precepts, issuing not so much directly from heaven as from a reflected heaven within our own bosom—not so much from GOD alone as from GOD reigning on the throne of our hearts, seated at the springs of the active energies of the intelligence, the will, the affections, the centres of our interior life.

(2.) A second mode of furthering this great end is to cultivate the spirit of faith in the Unseen and the Impalpable; to put forth as it were the arms of the soul, in the longing to embrace the Presence which has entered into it, stretching out and expanding the whole being as it exhausts itself in the desire to grasp It, to cling to It, to keep It; to strengthen the tendency which grace implants; to rise above the conclusions of sense and reason into the world closing everywhere around us, which rests only on the truth of CHRIST and the revealing of the Spirit; and by such exercise to become the more ready to believe that more than we can think or feel or apprehend is passing upon us, within us, even while we are "troubled about many things;" that nothing is too great to believe possible of Almighty Power and Love. The hope of the Eucharistic life being fulfilled in us, rests greatly on the belief of such boundless possibility, on the living conviction that the sources of Infinite development are as a well-spring within us; and needful it is that such faith should grow, lest it be fulfilled in us as once fatally of old, "He came unto His Own, and His own received Him not," while yet "as many as received Him, to them gave He power to become the sons of GOD, even to them that believe on His Name."[1]

(3.) The third practical suggestion is special devotion to the HOLY GHOST as the organ of the Godhead in the

[1] S. John i. 11, 12.

communication of the Divine Humanity. For He first ministers the grace of consecration, causing the Body and Blood of our LORD to be present, then next reveals Him to the soul, opening more and more of the Mind of JESUS as the soul is able to bear it, infusing into it, and interpenetrating it with the hope of that higher life of His Divine Humanity; and then communicates Him to those prepared to receive Him. He is still the Friend of the Bridegroom, Who prepares His way, and attends upon His movements, and rejoices in His Presence and His glory. It is indeed the joy of the HOLY GHOST, to communicate CHRIST and help to perfect the union between Him and the soul of His elect, leading the Bridegroom to the Bride, waiting and ministering till the union become more and more perfect.

Blessed SPIRIT, ever giving out Thy life for others, and ever rejoicing in another's joy, content if only the object of Thy Divine Mission be accomplished, and then only retiring that Thou mightest have nothing of Thy Own, Thy sacrifice of Thyself as complete as the offering up of the Eternal SON, Who sends Thee to us from the FATHER! Special devotion to Thee is the drawing out of our desires as a response to Thy Own, that Thy grace in return may be enlarged, and shed forth more and more abundantly as the joyous ministry of Love!

(4.) The further grace to cherish, which is also the secret discipline that strengthens and refines the soul, that it may correspond with the heavenly visitation, is patience—patience with our own weariness in waiting; with the hardness through which our stubborn natures are being broken down; with the necessary slowness of our progress because of our incapacity for grace; with the order of the Divine dispensations in His individual dealings with us, because He gives "grace for grace," restraining His greater abundance till His former gifts meet with a truer response and a profounder gratitude.

We need to exercise ourselves in these things, that our "profiting may appear unto all," but most of all to Him Who watches ever most keenly with His steadfast gaze, Whose honour is concerned in the faithfulness of those to whom He has trusted Himself, in whom He seeks to find a fitting resting place.

Alas, for the sad and desponding heart! If for the bright and hopeful it is difficult to realize the Indwelling Presence, and the sacramental powers working in us, because of their strangeness so foreign to our proper nature, what must it be to one lacking in faith, and downcast amid the mists and vapours that ever hover around this earthly state, and cloud the shining of the heavenly light!

But note what is really the cause of this self-engendered hindrance. It is not the infirmity of a fallen nature, because it is the very fact of our fatal weakness even unto death, which brought down CHRIST from above. It is not that there are still lingerings of our former sins, for He enters in for the very purpose of cleansing us, and the blotting out the soul's stain is part of the miracle of mercy involved in His Presence. It is not unfaithfulness to the great Gift in former times, for there is an ever fresh complete fulness in each Communion which obliterates the neglects of former Communions. All such hindrances only plead the more powerfully, the more touchingly, because of the greater need, and such hindrances are "common to man." He finds them alike in all to whom He comes, varying only in degree. The real hindrance more commonly, at least in the faithful and devout, arises out of the soul's tendency irrespective of any positive evil, but aggravated by such evil—the tendency to brood on its own defects, till it loses itself in its self-contemplation, sees only itself, and loses the vision of its LORD, Who is still within it, though hidden, or sees His Face only distorted or perhaps looking angrily through the darkness, as orbs of light are seen through the stormy clouds which the lower levels of the earth's surface generate. The hindrance is the soul's own persistent shrinking from the free, generous benevolence of GOD; the reluctance to cast itself on the all-forgiving, all-enduring, all-reconciling love of our LORD; the difficulty of comprehending the amazing truth of the possible co-existence of His Infiniteness with the littleness of the creature; of such a life as ours with the awful nearness of Him Whose "Name is Jealous," before Whom "the very heavens are not clean." Fears, scruples, self-accusings, self-complainings, distrusts, doubtings, pass rapidly across the face of the soul, agitating, perplexing, filling it with irrepressible anxieties, at variance with the dictates of faith, overmastering them, till it sinks down spent and exhausted with the vain struggle, till it lets go its hold and gives itself over as lost, while yet it acknowledges the boundless love and exhaustless compassion of its LORD towards others, towards all but itself; it dies to faith and hope while honouring GOD in others, and even thinking to honour Him the more through the self-abandonment of its own despair.

How can such a soul be aided in its sore distress, the increased strangeness which the Sacramental Life must present to such a one, a soul perishing even while help is close at hand, come on purpose to give aid at the instant need, more ready to grant than we to pray? One remedy is to lean one's own failing faith on the more trustful, assured faith and convictions of others, so that the spirit of faith may communicate itself to the sad and darkened spirit by a mutually organic sympathy. As the palsied man had need to be " borne of four," and so let down through the roof at the feet of that strange Presence of healing power, around Whom the world in its helplessness and amazement crowded, and was healed through their confidence, their faith, indeed, not supplying what his own lacked, but quickening and enabling him through the force of their sympathy and perseverance,—even so one soul may strengthen another, as it may intercede for another; and borne on the outward trust of another's stronger faith its own feeble energy may be enabled to rise.

The faith of ages, the witness of the Catholic Church of all time to the sure abiding Fulness of the Presence of our LORD, and all His powers of forgetting and forbearing love, may become the groundwork of a trustful childlike assurance, before the face of which all doubts and fears will vanish away; or even in the very worst estate of paralysed despondency one may constrain another to wait on in patience, like the poor cripple of Bethesda, beside the streams of healing, assured how others have found health and reviving, and that if the sufferers only wait patiently long enough by the spot where the healing virtue moves, more than the angel's presence will at length be felt and seen, the Eternal approaching the chosen soul, will surely at last be known, His voice be heard, and the unquestioned sense of personal individualising love will penetrate the enfeebled consciousness, filling it as with the rekindling of the first love, the thrilling joy of restored health. The remedy of the disease of ages may be the work of a moment, or even if this cannot be, and the soul is so helpless, so incapable of rising to meet Him as He approaches, yet still if one but cry, though only as the blind man by the wayside, he may be assured that at last his SAVIOUR will pass by, the cry will reach Him, the spirit of constant desire will draw Him to the sufferer's side,—" He will surely come, He will not tarry." And even though all be strange and dark, and Eucharistic truth fall listlessly as an unknown tongue upon the ear, and there is no understanding, no heart to apprehend the darkening mystery, and one stand alone among the unbelieving and the careless, the world around seeming only to confirm and countersign the collapse of such fondly treasured hope, vainly struggling with a general unbelief, one may still cast oneself on the conviction of the Apostles, who when all left Him yet still lingered by His side, not that they could see and comprehend the mystery of the sacramental life, but because they felt that He must be true, or truth must cease to be, that if He were false there could be none in heaven or earth to trust: "LORD, to whom shall we go? Thou hast the words of eternal life."[1] And yet the very craving of their souls for life was proof indestructible that He Who made them willed such cravings not to be in vain. However dark His words, however veiled His Presence, however hidden the promised bliss, they would wait in trustful rest of pure faith on Him Who promised, till in His own time He unveil His Face, and light spring out of the darkness.

[1] S. John vi. 68.

Nor will He fail such as trust in Him. He will fulfil His own purposes, for it was the very accomplishment of His one great design of giving Himself to such as trust in Him, that brought Him forth from heaven. "God so loved the world that He gave His only-begotten Son, that whosoever believeth in Him should not perish, but have everlasting life."[1] The long, almost despairing waiting for a blessing, may seem, as it were, to be all fulfilled at once. There may come the tide of the fulness of Life and Light and Joy, rushing in through the whole being. Though He may will us to wait during long periods of time, even years of painful expectation and suspense, yet He can cut short His work at last, and accomplish all His Will, as in a moment. His Predestination must fulfil its course. He may will to be glorified all the more after the long waiting. The morning joy is all the brighter because of the lingering of the night. The flood tide rises the higher when the ebbing is the lowest. The most brilliant sunshine is after the passing of the storm. God seems to delight in contrasts, as we call them. The changing of His hand, to us so startling, may be simply a necessity of His greatness. Life and Death touch each other's confines with a rapidity that must ever startle, and yet the interchange remains an abiding law. So learn we to wait His time, nor ever cease to trust Him. The very helplessness we feel, may be but the prelude to some more amazing manifestation of His love.

O Lord, Whose Name is secret, work in us the conviction that Thou art still our own, and though life itself sinks within us, and we seem passing into the nothingness out of which Thy hand was stretched forth

[1] S. John iii. 16.

to draw us into being, and all around grows dark and confused, yet Thou art GOD, and there is none other, and Thy word endureth for ever in heaven, and we cast ourselves on Thee. "Thou wilt keep him in perfect peace, whose mind is stayed on Thee, because he trusteth in Thee."[1]

[1] Isa. xxvi. 3.

XIV.

THE WORSHIP OF THE DIVINE PRESENCE.

We have dwelt on the exceeding joy and wonderful powers of the mysterious life which flows into us through the intimate union which the mercy of God hath wrought for us through the Blessed Sacrament, as the means of perfecting His Elect in Himself. We have hitherto dwelt chiefly on this Mystery with reference to those who communicate, and seen their inestimable gain, their mysterious joy, and how it is to be secured. But is there then no benefit for those who are present without communicating? Are we to limit the blessedness of the Sacrament to those who partake, and is there no inward joy or special work of love between themselves and their Lord in those who, though ordinarily partakers of Him, yet, whether from not venturing to approach so often, or from passing hindrance, desire to draw near to Him without actual reception of the awful Gift Itself?

Surely when we call to mind the words of love from our Lord's Own Heart, that His desire is to be " among the sons of men," and to " dwell in the habitable parts of the earth;" and hear Him saying to all, "I will not leave you comfortless, I will come unto you,"—thus speaking evidently of the companionship which, though withdrawn from sight, He longs to be evermore continued with His Elect; and moreover consider what it cost Him to separate Himself—the wrench, if the expression may be allowed, it evidently was to Him, as the terms of Holy Scripture testify, when He was constrained to leave the disciples at the 'hour of His Ascension,[1]—we may, pondering such expressions, gather from them that one part of the Divine Institution, beside that great purpose of communicating Himself to be our inward hidden Life, was the continuance of that felt nearness of intercourse, that sweet consciousness of companionship, which otherwise would have been lost and for which the human heart ever yearns towards those we love, a consciousness independent of any act such as Communion implies. Such a purpose would be accomplished by the appointment of a visible form notifying His Presence, even though Himself could not be seen. Actual sight is not essential to the feeling of the nearness of those we love, whose treasured memories are borne fondly in our hearts. It is not merely when we actually see them that our souls are filled with delight in the sense of our being with them and they with us—the least accustomed sign of their presence is enough to awaken the whole train of loving, restful, delighted thoughts, in which we live with them. We enter the house where one whom we love dwells, and at once the look of everything within assures us of him, that he is near, and the heart is at rest. All objects speak of his presence—the chair, the open book, the implements of daily familiar use, tell at once the

---

[1] See especially S. Luke's account of the scene: "And it came to pass, while He blessed them, He was parted (διέστη) from them, and carried up into heaven." The words imply a separation, as if by force.

whole story, bring at once before the mind all the precious associations that gather round the thought of the loved person: he lives before us in vivid substantial reality, through the power of association. And the feeling that at any moment he may appear only adds to the pleasurable sense of close fellowship which we experience from the unmistakable signs of his nearness.

This same universal law of our nature necessarily rules our consciousness also in the case of the Blessed Sacrament, for our LORD laid hold of this instinct, a law of His own implanting, in order to fulfil His promise of continued companionship, when it became no longer possible for the outward eye of man to behold Him. He would still be near to the soul He loves, and satisfy its cravings by the fullest possible enjoyment of that fellowship. And He effects it by means of the actual sight, not of Himself, which could not yet be and ourselves live, but of the signs and symbols which His Word has sealed to be the means of recognizing His Presence, assuring us that where they are, there He is, there we can hold sure converse with Him.

When we behold those outward signs, Himself is proved to be there. We are at once entranced and filled with this consciousness, and the mind is satisfied and absorbed as at no other time; and this may be independently of the Communion which follows. He is there, and the assurance of the visible symbols is enough; it is the certain pledge of our sacramental relation to Him. Communion is necessary for the actual felt embrace of Himself within one's own self, but without this we may have the satisfaction of the feeling of our being near to Him, and His being near to us. At any moment He might suddenly appear. If He willed He might instantly break through the veil which screens Him from mortal eyes, and in bodily substance His Form, His Face, stand out to view, where the covenanted signs of His Presence are.

During the time that we are wrapt in love before these outward symbols our assurance is the same as if we actually beheld Him with our bodily eyes. Our consciousness of what He is to us, is as unquestioned, yea, rather far more, than what *they* saw or felt who beheld Him under the veil of that Body of His humiliation, which hid His inner life. What faith now mystically discerns, is relieved of all that marred and clouded with doubt that glorious Presence, and is clothed with all the light and beauty which invest His Form as He is within the throne of GOD. Faith sees Him now in the heavenly glory in which alone He lives, as itself is kindled with the same light through His Spirit uniting heaven and earth, suffusing the Form beheld and the soul that beholds, with rays of the same glory.

Moreover, to be thus near to our LORD, even though we do not actually receive Him, cannot but be fraught with blessing. We read how they brought sick folk, and laid them down where the Apostles passed, that even "the shadow of Peter passing by might overshadow some of them," and become the source in some measure at least to them of healing power. Our LORD, as the crowd pressed upon Him, let pass through the very hem of His garment the virtue which healed the sick woman who touched it. An effluence was shed abroad around Him, emanating from Him, and passing upon those prepared to receive it. The savour of the sweet ointment was diffused beyond its own substance. Thus too "the Sun of righteousness" was to arise "with healing in

His wings." Around Him, beyond Him, wherever He moves, He reveals Himself. Effluences of light, and peace, and joy, are shed abroad, indirect effects of His nearness, over and above the fulness of life which from His Divine Person, possessed and possessing us, becomes our abiding joy. As by the stirring and hovering of wings there is shed out healing virtue, freshening streams of power, sweetness of Divine consolations, besides and beyond the gushing of Life proceeding directly from His Sacred Person. We can hardly but be stirred to quickened faith and tenderer love, as we pray before the consecrated signs of His Presence, His coming near to bless. What each may need He knows, what may gladden each heart is to Him a precious thought, and there may come some emanation from Himself which may supply that very need and reach that longing desire. Nor can we suppose that the soul which has thus approached, with its longings of desire and pleadings of its need, can go back from Him wholly empty and unchanged, when it has been so close to His amazing Fulness.

There, too, we may meetly prepare ourselves for the reception of our LORD, if unable at the time to receive Him. For however great our care to fit ourselves for a true union with Him, He Himself by His Spirit must prepare us. He Himself brings forth the wedding garment to clothe His guest at the Feast of Love. It is His FATHER's drawing which brings the soul to Him. His own attractions will bring out more and more in us of what will be pleasing to Himself. It is His Spirit cleansing it with absolving grace which removes all the hindrances, if any grave fault has intervened to check the confident approach, if the peace and rest of childlike trust needs to be repaired; and where the special absolving grace is scarcely needed, the abiding near Him for awhile cannot but reassure the soul that trembles lest it should too hastily draw yet nearer. To be breathing the atmosphere which His Sacramental Presence breathes; to cheer and gladden the soul with the brightness that surrounds the shrine of His abode; to be drinking in fresh resolves, quickened desires, purer aspirations and more vivid faith, where Angels and Archangels are folding their wings to adore Him in His earthly sanctuary, leaving even Heaven for awhile to do Him honour,—this cannot but be to catch at least something of the grace shed abroad from His Person, and to gain a deepened love making the soul more worthy when the time of actual reception is come.

There is for all in such attendance the opportunity of adoring our LORD, in itself the profoundest peace, and an elevation of soul which transforms earth to Heaven. To unite oneself with the multitudinous host of the Blessed who are adoring Him on the visible Throne of His Presence above, recognizing the Unity of His Person and the Reality of His Substance, the oneness of the veiled and the unveiled glory of the Incarnate GOD, as He adapts His earthly manifestation to our present state, while yet He leaves not His abode of ineffable Light where the Heavenly Hierarchies ceaselessly worship Him,—this is even now to be in Heaven. It is to honour Him for His own dear sake, without the benefit to ourselves which Communion gives. And it may be all the more pleasing to Him, because of the many profanations and irreverences of those who discern Him not, and pass Him by, or knowing Him to be there, turn their backs upon Him, or because of the lack of devotion in those who do discern Him and yet fail to pay Him that homage of praise which is His due. Love, if it were possible, would ever seek to repair the dishonour of the loved one. The very fact that He is disowned by others, quickens the desire to surround Him with additional marks of loving reverence. Our acts, indeed, can add nothing to GOD; nor can one creature compensate for, any more than he can redeem, another. We cannot repair a wrong done to Him, as though one's own offering of love could be accepted in another's stead, to supply the loss, or do away the wrong, or set another free. But love is generous, and the heart's desires have, because of love, a value which is not their own, when heart meets heart in mutual sympathy. And when again and again our LORD—as of old in visible Presence, so now in sacramental verity, —comes, and His own receive Him not, He must needs turn with satisfaction to those who count it joy even to be near Him, though they then seek no more, or draw not nearer, because they wait till their more perfect preparation has made them less unworthy. They come and tell Him what that interval of Communion has been to them, beyond all other times; how the longing for the Gift of Himself has grown with the growth of that Reception, how the increasing frequency of that wondrous Gift fills their heart with thanksgiving. They come and tell Him all this in His very Presence, and certainly it must be an act very pleasing to Him. To own our LORD when He mercifully comes to us, though we do no more, while the world proudly passes by, or canvasses with sceptical questioning the awful Mystery, as a mere controversy of the day, on which men may choose their sides, while He withdraws not

His dishonoured Presence, in His longing to bless even those that turn away from Him,—this is surely an act of love all the more precious because there is so much to disappoint and grieve.

There is the yet further blessing which accompanies the prayer made over the great Oblation, the joining in the Eucharistic Sacrifice. But this needs to be viewed as a separate subject by itself, and has already been considered as a main part of the Sacramental Mystery.

It is a most precious thought, enlarging our view of the tenderness of the love of GOD, that when He would bless us He superadds benefits which seem unnecessary for the attainment of the particular end in view, but serve only to increase our joy, or magnify His goodness. Thus it is, as already observed, throughout nature. To the forms of inanimate things, besides what is needful for life and the exercise of their powers, GOD has added other features, made only for enjoyment or beauty. Such are, in the material world, the many-coloured petals fringing the productive organs of flowering plants; or, in higher spheres of life, the exquisite joys of pure friendship, and all the delightful adornings of form or movement, of voice or feature, which combine to give the real charm to human life, and yet are not needful for its support. So it has been in the institution of this great Sacrament; we see like signs, as we might expect, marking the Same Hand and the same blessed purpose. It was ordained for the special purpose of pleading the Sacrifice of Atonement, and feeding the Elect with the food of immortality. And to fulfil these objects would have been enough for life and holiness. But this was not enough for His love: not enough for the largeness of His purpose to bless. He would superadd to these blessings the secret joy which arises from the sense of His nearness objectively perceived, consciously felt, so as to impart to the yearning spirit the rest of assured belief in His companionship, notwithstanding all our unworthiness, so closely renewed from time to time; a companionship silent indeed and impalpable to outward sense, yet to the faith which can see beyond the outward form, one ever speaking of love, and desire, and the certainty of a perfect union hereafter, as though no other end were to be accomplished.

What more, blessed LORD, couldest Thou have done for Thy own Elect? What remains for us to ask, but that Thou shouldest so enable us by Divine faith and the inner sight of supernatural consciousness, that we may rise to a true and real perception of what Thou dost thus evermore consecrate to our use, through which Thou wouldest work out such ceaseless beneficence? O send out Thy Spirit, and raise us to the height of this great Mystery. May the sevenfold Lamp of Fire ever burning before Thy throne kindle us, as we adore Thee before Thy altar-throne on earth, inflaming our hearts, and enlightening them, that they may be enabled readily to catch something of the spark of flame from the fulness of the radiance so close to us, though veiled beneath such earthly and inadequate forms! Yea, blessed LORD! Thou Thyself must enable the powers of our senses and our inner perceptions to correspond with Thy most gracious purposes for us. Enable us so to correspond, as Thou drawest us more and more closely, that we may meet Thee thus coming to us. In seeking this, we are asking what Thou, O good LORD, desirest even with a greater desire, pleading Thy own Intention, pressing home on Thee Thy own purpose. For Thou seekest us, not we seek Thee. Thou hast said, "Seek ye My Face." It is only as a faint response to Thy own word, that we can say, "Thy Face, LORD, do I seek." We love Thee only because Thou dost first love us. Be Thou the Creator in us of a love that can meet Thy love, and then may Thy Presence bless our enkindled hearts with a fervour of affection glowing ever more and more in the fire that consumes all that is not of Thee, till we shine as Thou shinest in the Glory that fadeth not away for ever.

XV.

THE INCARNATION ILLUSTRATED.

WE have dwelt on the mystery of GOD vouchsafing to give Himself through the forms of earthly elements, in order to unite Himself with us. We have dwelt also on the consequences of this union of our own sinful selves with the Sinless, the Perfect, the Divine. We have dwelt, moreover, on the blessing, the grace and power, flowing forth from His Presence beyond Himself, beyond His immediate contact which even those in some degree may share who only worship Him, pleading the great atoning Sacrifice.

These distinct views of the Eucharistic Mystery have passed before our eyes, and disclosed some visions of the vast, exhaustless powers of this Great Sacrament. But further, independently of these its proper effects and objects, the Mystery has a most important use in quickening our understanding, and deepening our faith in the central doctrine of the Incarnation. And this is a matter of the utmost moment. For the Incarnation is the one only real ground of hope of rising above ourselves into GOD, of the union of the heavenly with the earthly, and thus of a higher life being formed in us, through the communication of the Divine Nature— the Source of those secret Mysteries by which we are transformed beyond ourselves into Itself. A quickened faith in this great truth is the result of meditation on the Holy Eucharist, because of the important resemblances between It and the Incarnation, proving the sameness of the Mind Which planned both mysteries. Because of the resemblances the one truth assists the other. The apprehension of the one quickens that of the other, each becoming more true to us, by observing a sameness extending to both alike; for the mind is greatly moved by analogies.

(1.) Firstly, note in both mysteries the intimate union of the Infinite and the finite. In the Incarnation the first cause of wonder is that He Who comprehendeth all things and is not comprehended of any—Who encompasseth, filleth, and yet passes beyond all, to Whose attribute of Infiniteness, we can give no real name, for the mind of man is unable to take in the very idea,—should tabernacle in a human body, should enshrine Himself in a contracted form which we could see with our eyes and embrace in our arms. That all the attributes which characterise the Infinite should be thus embodied within the Man, One like unto ourselves, growing in stature, and dependent on the aid of His creatures, is the difficulty to faith. But observe how precisely this same wonderful characteristic marks our LORD's sacramental Presence. He accommodates Himself to the poorest and least of outward material forms, contracts Himself so as to be intimately identified with elements which we hold in our hands and take into our lips, for there He is Himself in all the Majesty and Power of His mature State. The two extremes of being meet in One: in the one case, the Infiniteness of Godhead coalescing with the limited form of a fleshy nature, His Sacred Humanity; in the other, the GOD-MAN, in the perfection of both natures, with the species of bread and wine.

(2.) Another marvel attaching to the Incarnation is the union, without confusion, of two substances so diverse as those of the Creator and the creature, substances which can never assimilate, or lose their separate essential distinctness; for GOD cannot change. It is an inalienable attribute of Deity to be unchangeable. The Humanity of CHRIST changes. It increased in wisdom as in stature. It became spiritual, glorified, deified; yet It still remains only Itself. Its organs, Its desires, Its capacities, are still and ever must be simply human, creaturely—what we can, at least as to their kind, understand in some measure, because we are of the same nature. Equally the Godhead retains Its separateness, and will ever preserve Its Infinite distance, Its perfect simplicity of Being. And yet in CHRIST the Two Natures are so entirely One that They cannot be divided; they are truly spoken of as One, and act as One. The One Name, JESUS, implies the Godhead equally as the Manhood; for they unite in One Personality. It is as true to say that GOD died on the Cross, though death could only affect His Humanity, as it is to say that the Man, CHRIST JESUS, is from everlasting, though His eternal generation is confined to His Godhead.

The same mysterious identity of divers and unequal substances meets us in the Blessed Sacrament, the Elements being taken out of their natural order, and being Divinely possessed, become the channels and instruments of His Presence, yet retaining their own substance and attributes. For there are the two substances, the one heavenly, the other earthly; the one Divine-Human, the other inanimate. And these substances retain their divers qualities and attributes perfectly distinct one from the other. But yet, through the grace of consecration by the operation of the Holy Ghost, they are most truly one according to sacramental grace. They are present before us as one object, are spoken of as one, enter into us as one. It is equally true to say of the Bread, when consecrated, "It is our Lord's Body," as it is to say of our Lord, "He is the true Bread." In receiving the Bread we receive His Body. Through the assimilation to us of the one is the assimilation of the other. And yet the one remains natural, the other supernatural, the one earthly, the other heavenly.

In both cases alike this wonderful characteristic of the union of such divers substances and natures meets us, brought into such amazing proximity, nay, more than this, into such an entire co-existence of life. There is, indeed, this momentous difference in the case of the Hypostatic Union between God and man, the Incarnation of God, that the union is indissoluble, while in His Presence in the Blessed Sacrament the union is assumed only for a time, that He may through the means of the elements unite Himself with us; when this is accomplished, His union with them ceases. There is the further difference, that in the Incarnation the union is of a personal character, the Humanity being an integral part of our Lord's twofold Being; in the Sacrament the union is purely accidental, for a purpose, as a passing shadow might invest a substance, or as the clothing of a living person. The union is temporary, not enduring, sacramental, not personal; though allowing for such differences it is equally real and true.

(3.) Again, how great is the mystery of the Incarnation in regard to its infantine commencement, and its progressive growth from the earliest form within the womb to its perfected glory at the Right Hand of the FATHER! In the Holy Conception "the seed of the woman" was as truly, as perfectly united with the Eternal Godhead of the SON, as now in His perfect Manhood. The full stature of CHRIST is not more truly one with the Divine Essence and Power than it was with the secret "substance yet being imperfect," which lay silently, being "fashioned beneath in the earth." How impossible for us to comprehend the inward growth to maturity, the gradual development of the organs, of the bodily and mental powers, which were becoming thus eternally the attributes of GOD!

A similar mystery meets us in the Blessed Sacrament. For there is the overshadowing of the Same HOLY GHOST, the same power of the Highest, in a marvellous operation. And the result is but as a seed, a germ of life formed in secret. But it is the Same Person of CHRIST adapting Himself to our littleness, the Same Divine Nature in both cases alike uniting Itself with forms of being wholly dissimilar to Itself, the amazing Fulness of the Life of CHRIST contracted within the outward forms of the Sacrament. And thus this same Presence communicates Itself in germs of everlasting life to each separate member of the Communion of His saints, to grow up a fructifying power developing Itself in each to become the perfect man, the mystical reproduction of the Same CHRIST, become the Fulness of GOD in His own true Elect, yet each one in that blessed company preserving his own separate gift distinguishable from all others. The parallel is complete. The SON of GOD, Who became "the seed of the woman," to grow even as we grow, by slow stages from weakness to strength, from least to greatest of created Being, even the Same Redeemer, the Same Life of man, becomes continually in countless multitudes the infant germ of a new creation, to grow more and more into a very sameness of life, to be manifested at last in a like glory within the Light that enshrines the perfect Godhead, and be thus made one with It for ever, all developed from that one Sacramental Seed of Life into the full stature of the perfect CHRIST.

(4.) Once more, we trace a striking resemblance between the two cases, in regard to the hiddenness which marks them both alike. In the Incarnation the stumbling-block to faith is, how GOD should be on earth, speaking with human voice, acting with human hands and limbs, touching and being touched, face to face with all who came to Him, and come on purpose to reveal Himself, and yet to be neither seen, nor known, nor understood, even by "His own," or discerned, if at all, most dimly and slowly, and then but by a very few supernaturally illuminated. Most mysterious, too, is it that having been thus in the world, tarrying so long, He should have left so little visible, sensible track of His Glory, such a faint impression of His Presence, the outward still so overshadowing the inward, the world so overpowering GOD within it. It seemed as if Almighty Power had to give way because of the incapacity, the blindness, the pride of the creature—because of the vast immeasurable incongruities between the Divine and the human—because His thoughts and ways are not our thoughts and ways. And yet all the while He sought even as it were to force Himself on the consciousness of

M

those who discerned Him not, leaving everywhere before the eyes of all marks of His Presence, only withdrawing Himself, and age after age preserving the same amazing hiddenness, lest the manifestation should be for a greater condemnation.

The very same law is perpetuated in the Blessed Sacrament. So hidden is our LORD—not only His Divinity but His Humanity also—inscrutably veiled and shrouded from every sense, except the hearing of the words that announce the fact, so neglected and passed by, alas! often so profaned and insulted, that men more and more, stumbling at this stumbling-block, disbelieve the possibility of any Presence at all under such utter abnegation of all outward appearance.

Yet what is this but a very repetition of His manner of intercourse with His creatures during the thirty-three years of sorrow in His first coming? What but the Same JESUS loving the same hiddenness?

And yet, beneath this secret hiding of His Presence—as in the days of His ministry, though despised and humiliated, at times He revealed His Power, even to alarm and confound His adversaries, as when the soldiers who came to seize Him fell helplessly to the ground before Him,—even so in the Blessed Sacrament, though neglected and profaned, His Power is so instinctively felt, that the wicked are terrified at His approach, the most careless shrink with conscious awe from receiving Him.

Nor is it less true both of the Incarnation and the Blessed Sacrament, that while the Presence of GOD is thus acknowledged and felt, Its hiddenness is preserved with the utmost jealousy, so that to seek to approach too near is to run the risk of losing what we have embraced, if not to suffer from the too daring attempt. Its law is hiddenness and mystery, only making Itself known to the inward senses, not to the outward, revealing Itself only to the souls of those who can "discern" Him. The creature must reverence the concealment of Him "Whose Name is secret." If we attempt to define too accurately, to examine too curiously, the mind becomes confused. The cloud is drawn around the mount. The very vision which faith had apprehended floats before the sight, vanishing from the grasp. It is an equal mystery in either case. GOD avenges His Secrecy, the sanctity of His veiled abode, while He penetrates the inmost sense with an indefinable awe.

JESUS is "the Same yesterday, to-day, and for ever." How marvellous that this great truth should be thus constantly manifested, as link upon link of a long chain, beginning with the wonderful manifestation which broke upon the eyes of the Apostles, which in that Upper Chamber was the Consolation of their fears, the Soothing of their bereavement, the Pledge of an after meeting, when they were about to lose Him for the remainder of their earthly pilgrimage,—that even while He is with the FATHER, fulfilling at an immeasurable distance the last great office of His Priesthood, He should still perpetuate on earth His Presence after the same laws; that His love continues to extend His Incarnation through a Sacrament characterized by precisely the same conditions that uniformly marked His life, thus giving the surest palpable testimony to the truth of the greatest work of His love; that He Who once appeared visibly to mortal eyes is with us still, after a like manner, though unseen, to unite us to Himself; that He who now feeds us with the food of immortality is the same that lay concealed in the womb, and hung upon the Cross—the Same GOD once humiliated, now glorified, yet ever concealed till the purged eyes of the perfected soul can dare to look on His unveiled Glory, and live. If angels and saints in bliss have a joy beyond our joy, as they gaze upon His Face in His visible Majesty, yet we on earth have the assurance that we are looking on the Same Form, to faith revealed; for the signs of His Presence are the same, the marks by which He is known are one and unchanging, revealing Himself to us as to them, though under a different form. Amazing love! that must part, and yet would not be parted; that must be gone, and yet would remain with Thy earthly ones; that must go and put forth the Fulness of Thy Life in that world in which alone Its Fulness can be developed, yet would abide with us under this contracted Form, that we might not lose Thee.

Most wonderful love and power meeting together in ever perpetuated Mystery! When Thou shalt come as Thou hast promised—the long expected, long waited for,—in Thy unclouded, undimmed Countenance, how will the long line of Eucharists which age after age have told of Thy Presence, yet concealed Thy Beauty, rise up to memory's gaze as they pass into the full revelation of Thyself of Whom they have been the assured, the faithful witnesses! What shall be the wonder of that Day, when the eyes of those who all their life long fed upon Thy Presence here on earth, shall see Thy Form unfold Itself, the Communion, which had so long been their rest, their joy, losing itself in the fulness of the beatific Vision of the SON of GOD and Son of Man, in His accomplished Fulness.

O LORD GOD, we pray Thee, so draw us to Thyself,

so attract us by Thy grace constraining us, so rivet our heart to know Thee here by faith, that as we grow upward in the constant reception and adoration of this great Mystery, we may be fitted for that Vision, when the veil shall be taken away, and Thou shalt be seen even as Thou art, and we become transformed even as Thyself.

XVI.

THE MINISTRY OF THE HOLY SPIRIT.

HITHERTO in considering the Blessed Sacrament our attention has been confined mainly to our LORD, and indeed to Him necessarily our view must always be principally directed, because it was instituted by Him specially for this purpose, that He should be ever present to us, projected, as it were, out of eternity into His earthly kingdom, that He may reign within it, and in the midst of His own Elect take up His secret abode. But it would be an imperfect view of the Love of this great Mystery, and Its stupendous grace, if we were not to embrace in our thoughts the constant and merciful co-operation of the Third Person of the Ever-Blessed Trinity in the same Mystery.

It has been observed, how all the acts of the SON of GOD, whether in His Incarnation or in His Sacramental Presence, are the consequences of His Mission, i.e., the outflowing of the Godhead into creation beyond that Presence in power and essence, which is in all things that exist by the Will of GOD. As there is a Mission of the SON of GOD in the world, so there is a Mission of the HOLY SPIRIT co-extensive with the Mission of the SON; the separate Missions of the two Blessed Persons being alike in some respects, though unlike in others. They are alike in their **extent** of operation, in their oneness of aim, in the perfect concordant energy with which the ends They will to work out are accomplished. But They are unlike in their manifestations and modes of operation. These differences and these resemblances alike, extending to the whole sphere of the Life of the Incarnation and the kingdom of grace, may be clearly traced in the Blessed Sacrament.

Our faith would therefore be imperfect, and fail to apprehend the Divine Love in its fulness, if we do not carefully consider the Presence and acting of the Blessed SPIRIT, and seek to "discern" Him, even as we "discern" our LORD. True, the HOLY GHOST is hidden, even as our LORD is hidden, and even more secret still is the hiding of the SPIRIT's Presence. For what we feel, the sensations which follow the participation of the Divine Communion, is a consequence of our LORD's imparting Himself to us, the effects of the virtues of His precious Body and Blood, and so of Himself, shed abroad in us. We specially receive our LORD as the "unspeakable Gift" of the Blessed Sacrament. A comparatively open and perceptible Presence is His Who is one with us in our very substance. But this "Gift" is due to the SPIRIT's power. The HOLY GHOST is the Worker of the Mystery, the Maker of the Sacrament. It is He Who unites the earthly and the heavenly to constitute the Sacrament. He rejoices in this union. It is He also Who, by His operations of grace within us, enables us to partake to our soul's health. He is therefore present throughout the whole Mystery, ever ministering. It is our LORD Who is given to us, but He is given only as the HOLY GHOST ministers Him to us, and ministers in us towards Him.

There is something peculiarly and most touchingly

beautiful in the hidden character of the HOLY SPIRIT's Presence in the Sacrament, hidden from the faintest possible consciousness, because our LORD is the One prominently brought out to view, to be sought, to be adored, to be offered, to be received. On this account all the deeper love, all the more thrilling tenderness, all the more tender reverence, are due; because He the Almighty, co-equal with the SON, condescends to exercise so entirely a ministerial part in the fulfilment of the Mystery.

But this is one special characteristic quality in the whole series of the operations of the Blessed SPIRIT, to be an aid and means to the Great End, which is CHRIST. It is His wont to withdraw Himself while ministering to another's glory, thus manifesting a lowliness of the profoundest self-renunciation. His ministering in the Blessed Sacrament is but the completion, in the same secrecy of love, of a long order of Divine operations intended to have the effect of uniting the Elect both in soul and body with JESUS. This mystery of His love and power may be traced from the very beginning. It began in the natural order of the world, when the HOLY GHOST moved on the face of the waters, bringing the new world out of chaos. He was then preparing the new mystical creation in its initiatory stage, laying its foundations in the material world, which He would gradually raise in the scale of being, until it culminated at its highest point of dignity in Humanity, in a form of being which might hereafter be made capable of union with GOD. The constant striving with the spirit of man, the illumination of the conscience through the earlier dispensations, the rebuking the power of sin in ceaseless judgments and warnings, thus raising the inner life to become capable of responding to a higher manifestation, and the creating within man ever-deepening longings and searchings of heart—afterwards, as time advanced, the inspiration of the prophets, ever enlarging the field of truth, and keeping up the constant growing expectation of the Incarnation of GOD—such was the preparatory work of the HOLY GHOST. When the fulness of time had come, Mary's birth and the grace which grew in her to such perfection, that she was fitted to become the shrine wherein Almighty GOD might take our nature unto Himself, was still His work, His overshadowing of Mary the crowning act of creative energy in raising Humanity into union with GOD.

After the Birth of the SON of GOD, now also the Son of Mary, the same SPIRIT still further developed His special work in perfecting the creation, as the Divine Humanity acquired ever fresh, ever more exalted powers. As "JESUS increased in wisdom and in stature," the HOLY SPIRIT was the secret Agent. In His Baptism openly the HOLY GHOST appeared in the form of the Dove, and thus in a manifested glory endued the Manhood of JESUS with preternatural gifts, which advanced His human nature to a higher stage of being. It was the Same SPIRIT "Who raised JESUS from the dead," shedding the glory of the Resurrection Life upon His sacred Body. Nor did His work cease—so at least we may believe judging from so many preceding instances of this great law of the mutual accordant operations of the Two adorable Persons of the Blessed Trinity—until, advancing upwards through the circles of ever-deepening light and glory, JESUS sat down, the perfected Man, at the Right Hand of GOD the FATHER. We may believe also that during those ten days which preceded the Descent of JESUS in the great sacramental mystery, the HOLY GHOST had His share in enduing His Humanity with those powers of self-extension, and all but ubiquity of Presence, which enables Him, without leaving His FATHER's Side, to be present, as GOD is present, according to His own Will, wherever the creative words which He ordained to be the crisis of the miracle of Love perpetuating His union with His mystical Body on earth, are spoken.

This long progressive series of Almighty operations, thus at last brought home to us, in infinite condescension and richest gifts of love, was the continuous going forth of the HOLY GHOST, His mission for the redemption and reconciliation to GOD of fallen man. While He was thus magnifying the SON of GOD, the SON of GOD glorified Him by announcing that this was His work, that He Himself was dependent in His Humanity on the co-working of the HOLY GHOST. JESUS often spoke of the results of the HOLY SPIRIT's work, as one with His own. Thus He said, speaking of His own Body, "It is the SPIRIT that quickeneth, the Flesh profiteth nothing."[1] He meant that His own Flesh, which was to become the life of the world, depended for its powers and influences on the SPIRIT's ceaseless energies; and His Humanity was, so to speak, nothing of Itself, could fulfil no purpose in forming the new creation, except only as acted upon by His SPIRIT co-equally, co-extensively co-operating with Himself; that as our LORD gave His Flesh to be the life and power of the New Creation, so the unseen SPIRIT had also His necessary part in quickening It, in investing It with

[1] S. John vi.

Deified attributes, making It the Centre and the Fulness of the perfected Communion of the Saints, even of all whom the FATHER, crowning the united work of the SON and the SPIRIT, first drew to Himself through Them, and hereafter will unite with Himself, so that GOD may become All in all.

This great truth of the operation of the SPIRIT in the Holy Eucharist is implied in words that occur at the close of the prayer which speaks of the great Oblation, the " sacrifice of praise and thanksgiving," when it is said that all is done " in the Unity of the HOLY GHOST." These words reflect back over the whole action, and are intended to awaken faith in His stupendous operation, the fulness of His co-operation, lest our souls should be exclusively absorbed and lost in love to Him Who comes to us more closely, more intimately still as He gives Himself to us, while yet His thus coming, thus communicating Himself, is only through the SPIRIT's agency.

As in regard to our LORD's Presence and the virtues of His Sacrifice, the HOLY GHOST is thus actively engaged, even so likewise in our preparation for receiving our LORD we owe our fitness to the same SPIRIT. He it is Who in our Baptism bestows on us the new nature which alone is capable of corresponding with GOD, and entering into spiritual relations with Him. He it is Who endues the regenerate with His sevenfold gifts in Confirmation, thus completing our capacity for union with CHRIST. Then, and not till then, are we capable of receiving CHRIST in the Blessed Sacrament. And why is this? Why is Confirmation necessary, but because we need to be raised above ourselves into a new sphere of being, and to be supernaturally endowed with living powers as the means of becoming substantially incorporated into CHRIST and CHRIST in us, in a new unity, resembling the union of the SON and the SPIRIT, from Whose conjoint action the sacramental mystery proceeds. It is not merely that the Life of CHRIST enters into us, but the SPIRIT of Life in us meets the SPIRIT of Life in Him. They are separate manifestations of the same Life, and the result of their union in us is the very formation and growth of CHRIST within our nature in His Image. It is the correspondence of our nature with the Nature of CHRIST through the Same SPIRIT Who abiding in us perfects the mysterious transformation, our being stretching itself forward to meet His perfect life-giving Presence, the Source of all perfection, oneself spiritualized meeting our LORD from Heaven in His living Glory.

We may take up our LORD's words, and say as truly in reference to ourselves—"It is the SPIRIT that quickeneth, the flesh profiteth nothing." The SPIRIT in us enables us to receive what the flesh is incapable of receiving. He endues the very flesh with spiritual capacities, and abiding in us becomes the living bond of communion with our LORD. He is the Love of the FATHER, and of the SON, according to the eternal law of love binding the Two in One. He is the union of the Divine and the Human in our LORD. By a wonderful condescension through an extension of a similar law He unites with Him in One Body His own Elect, reconciling the creature's unworthiness with the infinite perfections of the Incarnate GOD, revealing to him who worships, Him Who is worshipped,—to him who draweth near from below, Him Who draweth near from above.

Hence arises the need of careful preparation for the

reception of the Blessed Sacrament. In the old Sarum Liturgies it was directed that the Priest, while vesting himself before he approached the altar, should say the *Veni Creator*. A still more solemn rite occurs in the Eastern Liturgies, which also, derived from them, is introduced into the Scotch and American Liturgies. In connection with the Consecration Prayer there is, as an integral part of the mystical service, an Invocation of the HOLY GHOST, a direct petition for His descent upon the elements, to "make them the Body and Blood of CHRIST."

These directions were manifestly grounded on the principle above explained. There must be a coming of the HOLY GHOST first, and then through the HOLY GHOST the coming of the SON of GOD,—an advent of the SPIRIT Who quickeneth, and then a Presence of the Divine Humanity seeking an abode in hearts prepared by the SPIRIT to receive Him.

If there be any sin defiling us we cannot approach till that sin, through the grace of the SPIRIT, is cleansed away. We cannot of ourselves receive the Precious Body and Blood into ourselves—there must be a purification in order to receive them; there must be the SPIRIT's cleansing before there can be the power of reception. Nay, even when there is no such sin as hinders a peaceful approach to the Blessed Sacrament, there must still be a preparation to raise the soul's powers of apprehension, to expand its capacities and refine its senses, to quicken its longings, and reanimate its fervours,—there must be an increase of the SPIRIT, stirring up each one who approaches, to place the soul in accord with the glorified Humanity of the SON of GOD.

And surely the more frequently we receive there needs an ever increasing fitness; for the oftener our LORD comes to us to bless us, to assimilate His Life to our own, He expects to find an increasingly perfect welcome. As again and again He enters in, He looks to see more and more the effects of His coming. He cannot but take increasing delight in those to whom He is thus constantly drawing near, and He expects to find increasing desires and a purer love prepared to embrace Him. The bride is more beautiful, more lovely in the eyes of the Bridegroom, if she seek His love, and, longing for His approach, deck herself in attire which His taste approves. So must our LORD rejoice the more in one whom He sees growing more and more like unto Himself, in whom He finds the increasing reflection of His own attributes, the gratification of His own desires. His longing is for a closer union with His own Elect, and this growing union depends on the ever increasing likeness to Himself. But how can this likeness grow, except as the SPIRIT of CHRIST gives us more of His own Purity, His own Sanctity, His own preternatural gifts—as the SPIRIT which is One with CHRIST, of the same Mind with CHRIST, endows us with like gifts of grace, with like features of character, an unity of thought, a constant going on to perfection, even as He was "made perfect." Where mutual desires thus meet, and face to face the likeness of the features grows, each Communion is as though the one hastened to the arms of the other by the anxious drawings of a common love, which the Same SPIRIT of Love breathes alike in the Heart of the Bridegroom and the heart of the Bride, and breathes with fonder longings, as the time of the Marriage Supper of the Lamb draws nigh. The

Same Spirit that filled the Sacred Humanity of JESUS to be to us the Fulness of GOD, fits us to be capable of receiving that Fulness, even Himself Who is GOD and Man in One Divine Person.

O Blessed SPIRIT, shed abroad in Thine own Elect more and more of Thy wondrous Gifts. Stir their souls, kindling such preternatural fires that in their heat all remaining imperfections may be consumed. O hasten this fulness of our predestined sanctity. Raise our thoughts, our imaginations, to a higher strain, that faith fail not to embrace the amazing mystery; that CHRIST may be glorified in us, His own Elect, His love shed abroad in our hearts by the HOLY GHOST Which is given to us, that we may become a home of rest for our LORD's Presence to abide, never to leave, never to forsake us. May the wondrous Mission of the SON and the SPIRIT thus meet in us, thus accomplish in us that for which They ever and ever come forth from the depths of their own Eternity; to return into It with the gathered fruits of their ceaseless, boundless love.

XVII.

THE FULNESS OF THE SACRAMENTAL LIFE.

Some closing remarks only need to be added as to the view of our life taken as a whole, which the subject we have been considering suggests.

One main distinction runs throughout the kingdom of grace, separating more or less markedly those who are yet one in the possession of a common faith, the votaries of the natural and the supernatural life. By the natural life is meant that, while believing and resting on the Atonement of Jesus Christ as the only hope, practically the life is regulated in moral harmony with the circumstances of the social state in which the lot is cast. The supernatural life is that in which there is an apprehension of the highest truth as a moving principle underlying all outward circumstances, and raising them, the soul itself developing its spiritual capacities through such an apprehension to the highest possible standard. A sacramental life is the completest and highest form of this higher life, it is the Divine Presence of our Lord impressing Himself on earthly things, and is carried out by His own working in us, Himself overshadowing, pervading, informing, directing us, and ourselves lovingly accepting, intelligently apprehending, sweetly yielding the will, the affections, to endure and fulfil what is impressed upon the soul by the inner Divine Presence. There may be a like belief in the atonement, in the Presence and operations of our Incarnate LORD through the SPIRIT, in the grace imparted through sacraments creating and sustaining that life. There may be also more or less of a common belief in the objective Presence of our LORD under the external forms of the Blessed Sacrament. And yet the results of such faith greatly vary in the two cases.

The difference appears in the practical hold which the mind gains of the reality and personal influence of the Divine Presence. A sacramental life is the proper result of a true belief in the sacramental Presence of GOD. But there may be a want of apprehending the Divine Presence as a living, life-giving reality; or it may be regarded as a communication of grace without the consciousness of personal union; or as an object of adoration without the approximating and assimilating faculty which connects the Gift with the Giver, or the soul's active life with the Indwelling Presence. There may be the want either of that vivid clearness of faith which is "the substance of things hoped for, and the evidence (the practical realization) of things not seen," or there may lack a true appreciation of the proper effects of the Divine Communion.

We are in truth ourselves parts of a great sacramental system; for our whole present life and our own present state are but outward forms of a mysterious Indwelling of GOD, working out the ultimate reconciliation of all things to Himself by an accommodation of His secret Life through the SPIRIT, under temporary conditions of outward nature, until the perfect redemption is accomplished. What is fulfilled in forming the Blessed Sacrament Itself is an expressive representation of what through It is to be fulfilled in us. Hereafter we shall be wholly spiritual; the soul and body alike will be so assimilated to the Divine Nature, that the outward form will comparatively pass away, or rather the outward will be transfigured wholly into the inward, even as the Holy Eucharist will pass into the beatific Vision. But for the present, under the outward forms of a nature not as yet reconciled to GOD, the true life of the spirit is hidden, and works only as an inward spiritual grace. But to work according to the purpose of GOD the inward Presence must become a pervading, ever-animating life; and to judge of the intended effects, we must ponder the law which determines the nature of the sacrament through which He works. The result of His Presence in the one case exemplifies the intended result in the other.

We have seen how the sacred Presence of our LORD impresses itself on the mere earthly elements, identifying Himself with them, thus giving them a new character and a new name, and powers of a wholly different kind, making them simply His instruments for the fulfilment of His own purpose, organs of His infinite Life, and therefore, most sacred, to be consumed in the sanctuary guarded from all risk of profanation, kept for the one end of revealing and conveying CHRIST, and then, their work done, passing away.

A sacramental life is the transformation of our frail human nature after a similar law of subordination to grace, of yielding oneself to the full possession of GOD. It is the recollection of the presence of our LORD Who has entered into us, and of what He claims of us, and the thought of oneself as the intended embodiment of

His living operations, and the use of all our faculties and powers as instruments of His informing mind; and as the result, a sanctity which involves earnest discipline of the senses and inward powers, not for one's own sake only, but for the sake of our Indwelling LORD, Who would be dishonoured by their abuse, our life being preserved only that He may be glorified, all that is earthly in us to die and pass away as His Life in us is perfected. It is not that He is incarnate in us, but the result of His mission, if it were perfectly carried out, would be as though Himself had become to us what His Godhead is to His own Humanity; our state would be the reflection of the Hypostatic Union. His influence upon our thoughts, our words, our actions, would be like to His FATHER's influence on Himself during His earthly course. As He was "the express Image of the FATHER" to the world, even so our state would become the image of Himself, to be in the world as He was in the world.

Yet a notable difference is to be marked between the sacramental life of JESUS in the sacred Elements and in ourselves. His influence upon their outward forms is purely of His own will, as though a mechanical transformation of their inanimate substances took place. But in us there is the wonderful power of a willing correspondence with GOD; the inestimable privilege of an intelligent choice, a loving surrender of self, a ceaseless co-operation with Him. And this high dignity of voluntary self-renunciation is never to cease, so that every act is to be a continual offering to GOD, through the power of His grace, an ever ready response to His Will, the glory of a self-chosen captivity of love, while yet He Himself gives all the power of thus yielding to Him.

Nor does it detract from the reality because the service is imperfect. It may be defective, and yet it will be most real, if the whole bent and effort of the soul be true. Nor need the operations of this inward life be always consciously perceived. By the law of nature, whatever grows to be a habit, becomes from that very circumstance no longer an object of consciousness, as it was before; the several acts of which the habit is composed become undiscerned, unfelt. Nor even though we fail continually, and fall from a truthful co-operation with this great grace, does it follow that the reality of our union with GOD in this sacramental life is lost, however seriously it may be impaired. There will necessarily be involuntary weaknesses, failings from unavoidable helplessness or defect, temporary sinkings under the power of temptation, and even graver falls, over which the soul deeply mourns. Yet the very truth of a sacramental Presence of GOD implies an infinite condescension, a merciful accommodation of Himself to circumstances of infirmity and humiliations of our fallen state. It is a pledge of His bearing with us in our imperfections, of His forbearance towards our lingering faultiness, of His not leaving us even if we sin against Him, so long as we ever return to Him and repent.

Our LORD was Himself subject to the infirmities of our fallen state. He tasted the struggle with temptation. He was even oppressed by the loss of the consciousness of His true Life in the FATHER, under the desolation of the powers of darkness. But it was only a passing trial, a hiding of the Light of His Godhead, not a loss of Its Presence, nor any breach of the perfectness of union which enfolded His Manhood in His

Divine Personality. Sin He could not know. But all of human weakness, of man's close contact with sin, all of the loathsome spirit's horror, of defilement, of dismay, of rebellion, He for us learned by obedience to the sufferings of our fallen state. But all the while the inward Fulness of GODHEAD, even when the consciousness was clouded, was as complete in Him, as when It shone forth in the Transfiguration, or revealed Itself more actively in the Resurrection. And even so, though actual sin affects us as it could not affect Him, yet His "mercy rejoices against judgment," and sin is not imputed where the precious Blood is ever sought and ever applied, according to our need, and death is ever swallowed up of life. Beneath the clouds that pass across the Heaven of our life the same Light ever steadily shines, advancing to its meridian glory. The same love that reconciled us to Himself, "when we were yet sinners," will not forsake us if we stumble even to falling, while to Love we still cling; or if He forsake us it will be but in seeming, it will be to our consciousness only, to test our faith in the darkness, or to reprove us in the fear of the judgment, or to make the "silver lining" of the cloud shine out all the more brightly and more blessedly because of the transient eclipse.

There are chiefly three modes in which our LORD's Presence works upon us; His restraining, His directing, and His transforming power.

(1.) How little can we guess the amount of that constant action of restraint which the inward Presence of GOD is exercising upon our inward state. Think of all the evil that lies dormant in us, the lurking tendencies to all forms of sin, the excitable passions, the horrible fearful thoughts which might start up in us, the susceptibilities to the seductions of the world, or the flesh, the inclinations ever ready to array themselves against GOD and our better choice. What if any one of such powers were unloosed but for a moment? What desolation in the spiritual life, what profanation of the most Holy Place, the Sanctuary of GOD! What wasting of the strength of the spiritual life! What an account hereafter to be given! And yet against such fearful risk the Divine Presence must be ever silently acting; checking the evil tendencies, anticipating the incipient risings of passion, overmastering the enemy in his first essays. And to Him thus ever near we can appeal to put forth His power, more ready to hear than we to pray, a source of strength at hand, ever within us, to which we can turn for assured deliverance to put the evil away, or hold it down, while we trust and abide steadfast, enduring in this confidence to the end. Even in sleep, or in times of sudden pressure, or of distracting cares, when it is so difficult to preserve the discipline of thought, we may believe that He who guards us as His own abode, is still watching to keep us pure, to sustain our peace.

(2.) The directing informing influence of CHRIST, through His SPIRIT, is that which gradually raises the standard, and expands the faculties of the renewed nature, impressing His own Mind on the mind of His servant, and so forming the character of the revelation of Himself. It is a twofold consciousness of the continual working of our LORD Himself and of His Spirit in us. He said of the HOLY GHOST, "He shall take of Mine, and shall show it unto you." This high spiritual revelation is perpetually unfolding itself in one who is living a sacramental life, the SPIRIT enabling the soul to see more and more of its LORD; his inner character opening itself out more and more under the light of the SPIRIT's illumination, and enabling the soul to take in the hidden depths of the Blessed Nature of the Body of CHRIST into which we are being formed. And this embraces the inner world of truth equally as it does the world of saintly beauty, even the deep things of GOD coming out to view through the SPIRIT, " Who searcheth all things." Every single Divine Light of which the soul is conscious, every revelation of the Mind of CHRIST, is an instance of what is perpetually going on in us to form a sacramental life. Nor is there any limit to the development of the revelations of GOD within the soul where Himself abides, Who is given that He may "lead" CHRIST's own Elect "into all truth," showing even "things to come." For where, if not in the shrine of His own indwelling, to one who faithfully listens for His voice, may the fulfilment of His promise be counted sure? To this operation of grace is due all the growing wisdom and knowledge of GOD, and of heavenly things, which is at once the counteraction of the earthly tendencies of the soul, and the elevation of the inner powers of thought, as the new world, which in CHRIST has become our own proper home, opens to the gaze of faith.

(3.) There is yet a greater power at work within us in the actual transformation of our nature which tells on our whole being. For our LORD is present as a creative energy, or rather as one reconstituting our natural being after His own Likeness. His SPIRIT not merely reveals to the eye of faith the living truth.

The vision is given that it may form for itself a reflection of its own beauty in the very substance of the soul's life. He is as the potter moulding the clay, impressing the shape, the features of His own Image, and so forming a newness of life. He first reveals to the soul what His will is, what the grace which He Himself has embodied in Humanity. He then attracts the soul, awakening its desires, and quickening its energies for the attainment of the same perfection. But beyond this revelation of Himself follows the crowning grace of the communication of His own Nature, pervading the very texture of our being, changing its substance, and newly forming all its features to be as He is, to be like Him, to be one with Himself in the perfect accord of the same mind.

It is the very characteristic of this perfecting work of grace that, like Himself after Whose Image and by Whose mercy it is fulfilled, it is secret. As the inner powers of life throughout all nature grow imperceptibly, manifesting themselves only by their effects, so very specially is this the case in the profoundest sphere of nature's highest form of life, the heart of man. Undiscerned even by its own consciousness in its keenest sensibilities at all times is the operation of our LORD's Presence, even when most active and most effective. So secret is its working, that when we perceive within ourselves influences and movements beyond ourselves, yet we cannot distinguish them from the actings of our own nature. Even though our old nature dies, and forms of a higher mind take its place, "the life of JESUS becoming manifest in our mortal body," yet this higher spirituality will still assume the shape of our natural faculties and powers; it will be what is human still, though instinct with what is Divine. So truly the "inward spiritual grace" still wears the aspect of the "outward visible form." The law of the sacramental Presence of our LORD is still preserved throughout the economy of our present state, to pass away only when "death is swallowed up in victory," when "the day breaks, and the shadows flee away."

Nor could it be otherwise. For how could we bear our part, or fulfil our probation in this world, if we were conscious of the transcendental mystery ceaselessly at work within us? How could we mix in the unavoidable details of ordinary life; how take interest in any of its many claims and duties, still less in any of its lighter pursuits, which yet are evidently suitable to our state, if the awfulness of such a Presence were continually revealing Itself within our very bodily form? Still more, how impossible would it be that we should learn to live by faith in the light of such a preternatural consciousness; and yet "to live by faith and not by sight" is the essential condition of the trial, on which our future hope of blessedness in GOD wholly depends?

We must ever bear in mind that it is not enough to catch glimpses only of such a life as here, however imperfectly, is described. We can indeed have but transient revelations in its earlier stages. But as the "light of the just shineth more and more unto the perfect day," even so a sacramental life has its dawning, and its progress, and though but by slow degrees advances as the grace of perseverance is vouchsafed, the reward of "patient continuance in well-doing;" and as the steadfast faith deepens into an abiding vision, it becomes a second sight to the soul evermore fixed on its Indwelling LORD.

We may here remark two great means by which to cherish this life. One is an introspection, a looking to the Higher Presence in oneself. This is distinct from self-consciousness, and is in fact the corrective of self-consciousness. Surely if we believe that we have received into ourselves all the Fulness of CHRIST, all that is gathered up in His own Person, His Infancy, His Early Life, His Ministry, His Passion; all the Glory into which He has passed, in which He abides; if we feel that He in all this Fulness is thus abiding in us, we are not looking into ourselves, we are looking at that Higher Being Who is within ourselves, looking unto CHRIST where He is continually revealing Himself in our life. We can thus look, and speak to Him within ourselves. "Thou art in me, Blessed LORD! I will see Thee within my own being as Thou art in Thy own Being, and as I gaze the Vision opens before me, and I see the possibility of a new life for me, as I look on what that Vision reveals." This is one element of inward thought cherishing the power of a sacramental life.

Secondly, with this introspection, which is rather of simple faith in the Great Truth, there must be an inward communing in secret prayer, the seeking the influence of Grace flowing from the Divine Presence within us. "Oh that Thou wert more impressed upon me! Oh that I were more conformed to what I believe to be within me! Oh that there was in me more and more desire and earnest longing to be united with It!" As such desires become more and more the secret communing of the heart, the consciousness of the inward Divine Presence will grow, and the grace will flow forth in the soul.

Most Merciful! on Thy tender pity the believing soul casts its hope. To Thy love, more deeply comforting, more unfailingly sure, than ever was a mother's for her only child, the feebleness of the fallen spirit must ever cling, as its only stay. And Thou art our God, and all that we are or have is of Thee. And as Thou hast promised even this further grace to complete and crown all Thy former gifts, and hast inspired in us the desire, we trust that all shall yet be ours; for Thy Word has said, "all things are yours, whether the world, or life, or death, or things present, or things to come, all are yours, and ye are CHRIST's, and CHRIST is GOD's."[1] Nor need we fear while we are ever receiving the very Incarnate GOD into the depths of our soul; for "He giveth power to the faint; and to them that have no might He increaseth strength. Even the youths shall faint and be weary, and the young men shall utterly fall; but they that wait upon the LORD shall renew their strength; they shall mount up with wings as eagles, they shall run and not be weary, they shall walk and not faint."[2] For not to those only who saw the LORD in the Flesh, is this grace given, to live in the ceaseless consciousness of His Presence. For they who saw Him face to face, themselves "bear witness," and "show unto us that eternal life which was with the FATHER, and was manifested unto us,"—they still speak to us in the power of the Apostolic grace, saying to us of every place and every age; "That which we have seen and heard declare we unto you, that ye also may have fellowship with us; and truly our fellow-

---

[1] 1 Cor. iii. 22, 23.   [2] Isaiah xl. 29—31.

ship is with the FATHER, and with His SON JESUS CHRIST."[1]

To Him who has thus loved us, and in Himself given to us more than we can ask or think; to the everlasting Trinity, FATHER, SON, and HOLY GHOST, be all praise and thanksgiving for ever and ever. Amen.

[1] 1 S. John i. 2, 3.

www.ingramcontent.com/pod-product-compliance
Lightning Source LLC
Chambersburg PA
CBHW032133160426
43197CB00008B/630